Forever Friends

PAM BOYER

HARVEST HOUSE PUBLISHERS
Eugene, Oregon 97402

Except where otherwise indicated, Scripture quotations in this book are taken from the Holy Bible, New International Version, Copyright 1973, 1978, 1984 by the International Bible Society. Used by permission of Zondervan Bible Publishers.

Verses marked NKJV are taken from the New King James Version, Copyright 1979, 1980, 1982 by Thomas Nelson, Inc., Publishers. Used by permission.

The names of some of the people, places, and circumstances appearing in this book have been changed to maintain their anonymity.

FOREVER FRIENDS

Copyright © 1992 by Harvest House Publishers
Eugene, Oregon 97402

Library of Congress Cataloging-in-Publication Data

Boyer, Pam, 1953–
    Forever friends / Pam Boyer.
    ISBN 0-89081-958-0
    1. Friendship—Religious aspects—Christianity. I. Title
  BV4647.F7B694   1992   92-4834
  241'.676—dc20   CIP

All rights reserved. No portion of this book may be reproduced in any form without the written permission of the Publisher

Printed in the United States of America.

To all the

Forever

Friends

and teachers whom I

have gleaned from

through the years.

ACKNOWLEDGEMENTS

Without filling many pages with names I cannot properly thank all those who contributed through interviews, prayer, and encouragement. This book is filled with their lives and my love to them. To all of you who gave of your time, thank you.

To Linda Torquato, I give special thanks and much love, for without you this book would still be in my heart.

To Andy and Melody Green Sievright, I send my thanks for your support, encouragement, and love.

To Eileen Mason and LaRae Weikert, I give my love and respect for seeing me through this process and helping me keep my sanity!

To Dick Foth, president of Bethany Bible College, my thanks for allowing me to use the principles on relationship God has given you.

To Bob and Shirley Hawkins, for your love and friendship through the years and for seeing this book in my life.

To my precious daughters, Amy, Katy, and Annie, for sharing your mom and allowing me to use some of your life experiences.

And finally to my wonderful husband and my forever friend, Rich, for seeing more in me than I could ever see in myself.

Friendship. Making friends, keeping friends, and being a friend.

We tell ourselves something so basic should be simple to achieve. But in reality, our relationships are often complicated, frustrating, and even hurtful. Why is it so hard to build the fulfilling lifelong friendships we desire, and to be the kind of friend we dream of being?

The quick-paced society we live in today doesn't help matters either. How do we stay connected with each other when our lifestyles often leave little room to cultivate the people most dear to us?

Well, there *are* answers. And you're holding some of them in your hand right now.

God places a very high value on friendship. In fact, He created the whole world to revolve around friendships—first our friendship with Him, and then our friendships with others. God obviously finds great joy in relationships, and I believe it's a joy He wants us to experience as well. We were not created to be alone, so God gave us the gift of friends.

Our relationships speak loudly. The world quickly takes notice of "the difference" Jesus makes when it comes to friendships. When they see—and experience firsthand—friends who hope the best and refuse to quit loving even when it hurts, they get hungry to know the Source of such love.

When we look at it honestly, making friends is not as simple as we'd like to think. On the other hand, it's not all that complicated either.

Pam Boyer has been my friend for over 15 years. In that time we've been through a lot. Pam has stood by my side as I buried my late husband, two of our children, and my mother. She's also stood by my side during some of my most joyful moments—the birth of my fourth child, and most recently, at my wedding.

I am very excited about her first book because when it comes to friendship, Pam knows what she's talking about. I've seen her work these principles into her own life.

This book is filled with godly wisdom and insight as the whole spectrum of friendship is explored. Pam gives you ideas on how to make new friends and really get to know them. She also covers important topics like receiving criticism, extending forgiveness, handling conflicts, bringing out the best in others, overcoming prejudice, and going the extra mile. I think you'll appreciate Pam's honest and direct approach—and I know all of the interesting stories woven throughout this book will find practical applications in your own life.

Someone once said, "If you want to make a friend, first you need to *be* one."

Pam Boyer's book tells you how to do both.

—Melody Green Sievright
Lyndale, Texas

CONTENTS

Forever Friends

PART ONE

Growing a Garden of Friends

CHAPTER ONE

Are You in a Weed Patch or Garden of Friends?

Every childhood is full of life-shaping experiences. One of mine took place in my neighborhood at Cindy's house.

Several times a week I knocked on Cindy's front door to see if she could come out and play. Cindy's mother would answer the door and smile down on my chunky, freckled face framed by flaming auburn hair, hoping this innocent fifth grader could not detect her hidden agenda. "Cindy, Pam is here. But you can't go out and play until your room is cleaned up." She just as easily could have announced, "Cindy, your personal maid is here." She knew that Cindy would secure my services to help her clean up her room so we could play together.

I never objected. My dad's job caused us to move

almost every year, and I was starving for companion-
ship. So I gladly accepted Cindy's request to help her
with her room, which always looked like a devastating
tornado had ripped through it. Cindy was happy.
Cindy's mother was happy. And, even though I felt
used, I was happy just to have a friend.

After two hours of rescuing forgotten toys from
under her bed and rearranging the chaos in her closet,
Cindy and I had a grand total of 10-30 minutes to play.
Then her mother would deliver her familiar line, "Pam,
I think it's time for you to go home now." Of course it
was. Cindy's room was clean. My usefulness was at an
end until the tornado struck again.

I wasn't naive. I knew what was going on. But
somehow in my loneliness I accepted the routine because I desperately needed a friend.

The scenario was regularly repeated for about six
months. Then one day after the cleaning ritual, Cindy
gave a new definition to our friendship. We were standing alone together in front of her house when she said,
"Pam, if any other kids from school come over or ride
their bikes by my house when you're here, I want you
to disappear. I don't want anybody to know you're a
friend of mine."

Cindy the human tornado had just ripped
through my heart. Her words crushed me. I felt like a
solitary flower trying to bloom in a weed-infested
vacant lot. I wanted so badly to be planted in a garden
of beautiful, fragrant friends. But after being stung by
Cindy's nettlesome words, I was afraid to call anyone
my friend. As a result of my experience with Cindy, I
retreated into seclusion for the next two years.

Since then I have learned that a relationship in
which one person is a user and the other person is being used should not be filed under the heading of a

friendship. Sadly, more adults are involved in these user/used relationships than children. The only difference is that the adult Cindys of the world no longer need their mothers to initiate the action.

Frantic for Friendship

I am grateful to Cindy for one thing, however. Her strange concept of friendship launched me on a quest early in life to find out just exactly what real friendship was supposed to be. Even as a child and adolescent I pondered deep thoughts about friendship: What kind of friends do I want to have? What kind of friend do I want to be? What does it take to cultivate a garden crowded with loving, supportive friends?

Unfortunately, in the early years of my quest I came up with more wrong answers than right answers. I found more pain than joy in the development of my friendships. When problems would arise with a new friend, I simply crossed him or her off my list and moved on in search of someone else. I wasn't interested in working through conflicts. After all, why should having a friend be so complicated?

I knew God must have a better way. After all, didn't He announce that everything He created was good—except one thing: our aloneness (Genesis 1:31; 2:18)? We were designed for relationships with God and with each other. Togetherness is good. Aloneness is not good. Even society understands this principle. Misbehaving children are sent to their rooms—alone. Rebellious teenagers are "grounded," denied social interaction with their friends. Teachers send uncooperative students to "time out"—alone. When we punish lawbreakers, we separate them from their loved ones and confine them to prison cells. Nonconforming prisoners are placed in solitary confinement.

Yet, as I looked around, I noticed that I wasn't the only person hurting for true friendship. Despite what God said, caring relationships seem to be the exception rather than the rule in our society. This is not a modern phenomenon. It's been this way for some time. Ralph Waldo Emerson wrote over 100 years ago: "We take care of our health; we lay up money; we make our roof tight and our clothing sufficient; but who provides wisely that he shall not be wanting in the best property of all—friends?"

Even as a young woman I knew that Emerson was right. Nurturing caring relationships in our society is not a high priority. Many people are locked in self-imposed prisons of loneliness. Whole neighborhoods are characterized by people who share common property lines or walls but who hardly speak to each other. Kindness and consideration between neighbors is rare. My friend Linda just moved into a private, gated community in Southern California. She was shocked when two of her neighbors actually took time to bring freshly baked goodies to her door and welcome her to the neighborhood.

As a young Christian I yearned for some kind of personalization in an obviously depersonalized world. I wanted to be a name, not a number. I wanted faces to light up when I walked into a room. I wanted to feel accepted, not just tolerated. I wanted to be able to share my troubles with someone and feel safe, knowing I wasn't alone. There's nothing wrong with wanting to be acknowledged, loved, and accepted in a world that doesn't seem to care much about people. But, like many people, I didn't know how or why to be a friend.

By young adulthood I had logged several unsuccessful years at making close friends. I had to honestly examine what was preventing intimacy in my friendships from taking place. What were my expectations? I wanted a friend who was interested in me, who wanted to do what I wanted to do, who enjoyed what I enjoyed. I didn't think I was asking too much. Yet for all my years of seeking it seemed I had gained little more than a long list of disqualified applicants.

Growing a Garden of Friends

In one of those prayers of desperation we sometimes pray, I asked, "Lord, why can't I find someone to fit my qualifications for a friend?" His answer was soon very clear, as if He had been just waiting for me to ask: There were too many I's in my definition of a friend. Nobody could live up to my list of self-centered qualifications for very long. And when they failed me in some way, I dropped them. Like many of us, I was only equipped to cultivate a garden of friends with the rusty experiences of my childhood. Even though I never used anyone knowingly, I realized I wasn't much farther along in learning how to be a friend than Cindy, the human tornado from my childhood.

As long as people danced to my tune, our friendship was fine. But whenever they failed to meet my expectations, in effect I told them to disappear. I wondered how many true friends I had driven away in my young life because I was only interested in what they could do for me, not in what I could do for them.

Thankfully, God didn't leave me crumpled in a discouraged heap. The One who created us for loving, caring relationships directed me to His resource book for making and keeping good friends. I began studying

God's principles for friendship in the Bible and applying what I learned to my relationships.

Old patterns of behavior were not broken overnight. But instead of walking away from my friends when problems arose, I started working through those rocky times with them. These difficult experiences helped me grow stronger as a person and learn to see things and people differently. And as I learned to persevere the trials of nurturing relationships, I developed character traits that others were looking for in a friend. The cycle perpetuated its own momentum. The more I sought to be a caring friend, the more caring friends I gained. My quest for friends has turned into an adventure of a lifetime. This adventure has filled my life with more friends than I could have ever imagined.

I picture my life as a garden and every friend as a beautiful, distinctly unique flower. I have collected many different varieties of friends in my garden over the years. Some are like tea roses. Their sweet fragrance lingers long after we've been together. Other friends are stately and dignified, like bird of paradise. A couple of my friends resemble the exotic orchid. Just knowing them is a rare pleasure. Others are like sunny, everyday daisies. They're just comfortable to be around. And a few are like the prickly pear cactus. They try to keep other people at arm's length and must be handled with special care.

I have a dual role in this garden of life. I am a flower, hopefully bringing as much beauty and fragrance into my friends' lives as they bring into mine. But I am also a gardener in my garden. I am responsible for cultivating and nurturing my friendships. Learning to tend my garden of friends and seeing the results has given me confidence that friendships *can* last through time. Over the years the fragrance of my garden has become sweeter, the colors more vibrant.

Perhaps in your experience of friendship you have felt more like a feeble volunteer choking in a neglected garden than a lovely flower thriving in the glory of well-tended soil. Maybe you've had some Cindys in your background who stunted your growth. Maybe you've been a Cindy yourself in the lives of others.

Let me encourage you. God has planted you in a garden of potential friends. All around you are people whom God has called to bless you and to whom you have been called to be a blessing as a friend. Remember: God didn't create us to be individually potted plants sitting alone and apart on distant window sills. He created us for relationship. He created us to be a garden. You simply need to understand and apply His principles for nurturing true friendship.

That's why I wrote this book. I want to share with you what I have learned and applied from God's Word about developing and maintaining caring relationships. God's principles will definitely help you "bloom where you're planted" as a friend. But more importantly, these guidelines will equip you to become a loving, nurturing caretaker who can help others bloom in the garden around you.

For the Love of a Friend

Before we launch into specific principles for friendship, we'd better agree on a general definition for friends. My good friend Nancy says that a true friend is someone who loves you in spite of yourself, just because you're you. You don't have to try to be someone else or put on a front. When you're having a bad day and don't want to talk to anyone, a true friend will understand and give you the space and time you need—and maybe a hug.

Another close friend of mine, who lost her husband in a car accident, expressed the same idea. She said her friends were those who understood her times of silence.

My favorite definition of a friend, however, is this: "The one who comes in when the whole world has gone out."[1]

This definition parallels the Bible's picture of friendship. Wise King Solomon wrote: "A friend loves at all times" (Proverbs 17:17). Jesus declared: "Greater love has no one than this, that he lay down his life for his friends" (John 15:13). God defines a friend simply as one who loves not primarily in an emotional or physical way but in a godly, giving way.

We often define friendship by what we *get* out of it: someone to give us space, minister to our needs, stick with us through thick and thin. But God defines friendship by what we *give* to it: allowing others space, ministering to their needs, sticking with them through thick and thin. That's why the chapters ahead emphasize our role as caretakers in our garden of friends, teaching us how to nurture friendships.

In our definition of friends, we're talking about unconditional love, the same kind of love God exercises toward us. God is no respecter of persons, and He doesn't allow His children to be either. Unconditional love does not depend on who is receiving it: casual friend, close friend, family member, stranger, enemy, Christian, or non-Christian. As far as God is concerned, we are to treat everyone the same (Luke 6:27; 1 Thessalonians 3:12). Nor does it depend on how these persons treat us or don't treat us. Unconditional love is freely given—no strings attached.

The wonderful part about loving unconditionally is we shed those inner restraints that keep us from reaching our fullest potential as true friends. We start becoming more like Christ. Unconditional love even frees us to be our own best friend. We stop thinking in terms of fulfilling the expectations or conditions other people tend to place on us.

Unfortunately, most friendships flounder in the quagmire of earned love. Earned love offers friendship with a conditional clause: I'll be your friend *if* you'll be mine; I'll be your friend *as long as* you do what I like; I'll be your friend *until* you no longer meet my needs. Cindy was my friend *as long as* I helped her clean her room and disappeared when her other friends came around. And I was her friend *until* I was tired of feeling used.

But deep inside we all want to be loved just as we are. Isn't that why we were so attracted to Jesus? He loved us when we were unlovable (Romans 5:8). And He continues to love us unconditionally. The people around you are looking for the same kind of love. They want to be around someone who will love them unconditionally—without a performance rating, without having to prove themselves, without a payback. Loving our friends without conditions and with no thought of anything in return is a new way of thinking for most of us. But it is the secret of a satisfying long-term friendship.

Where do we start in our quest to love others unconditionally? We can only love others unconditionally when we acknowledge that in Christ we are completely loved and accepted by God. We must see ourselves as

God sees us in Christ. The best source for improving the way we see ourselves is the Word of God. The Bible tells us that we are made in God's image and that Christ loved us completely through His death and resurrection. The more you grow to accept yourself as the object of God's unconditional love, the easier it will be to love others unconditionally.

Unconditional love works progressively outward. First we must choose to see and accept how deeply God loves us. Then we can progress to loving our families, those closest to us. Next we will be able to love our friends and even our enemies. As we learn to live daily in the truth of God's love for us, we must daily choose to love others at every level of relationship.

Growing and nurturing a beautiful garden of friends takes time and effort. My quest for true friends has become a lifelong quest. I'm sure yours will be too. The principles in the pages ahead are not a quick fix to all your relationship problems. But they will launch you into a fruitful, long-term process for discovering and nurturing friendships. And the Creator will reward your labors of love in ways you never imagined possible.

CHAPTER TWO

How Does Your Garden of Friendships Grow?

Like beautiful gardens, friendships don't just suddenly appear. They usually begin very small, like seeds, and grow over time. The problem is that we want quick-rooting, fast-growing friendships. If we don't immediately click with a new acquaintance, we seldom consider looking for a tiny, hidden seed of friendship that can be cultivated over time into a healthy relationship.

As a result, we tend to gravitate toward "desirable" people who fit within our well-defined comfort zones. You can distinguish your comfort zone for potential friends whenever you walk into a room full of people. There are certain people you are drawn to because of their physical appearance, outgoing personality, spiritual maturity, ethnic or cultural background. And there are other people you tend to ignore because they don't immediately fit into your relational comfort zone. You give them only a passing glance while search-ing for "kindred souls."

What happens when you only nurture relation-ships with those in your comfort zone? You develop a limited concept of friendship. By automatically exclud-ing the people outside your zone, you may never know the blessing of some other potentially enriching friends. And they will miss the blessing of being friends with you. The first step toward growing a good friendship is recognizing the seed of friendship that resides within each individual and knowing how to cultivate it.

Going the Extra Mile to Make a Friend

The people you feel comfortable around are like seeds that are capable of germinating immediately if the proper environment is provided. It takes very little ef-fort to encourage these relationships. For example, you are introduced to someone at church or at a party. After only a few minutes of conversation you're saying to yourself, *What an interesting person she is! We have so much in common. I want to invite her over for coffee so we can get better acquainted.* Most of us cherish a number of friend-ships that sprouted and grew quickly in the warmth of common interest and mutual attraction.

While attending a birthday party of a friend of mine, I noticed one of the guests I didn't know. He at-tracted attention the moment he walked into the room. He immediately had an audience. He seemed to know the right things to say. And when he moved to the next room he had a new audience. People responded to him, and he responded to them. I found myself enjoying his company. He naturally challenged the other guests to have fun. He was the kind of person a lot of people would like to know as a friend.

Then there are those potential friends who exist outside your comfort zone. These people are like dormant seeds. Friendship with them can be just as rewarding and enriching. But it doesn't happen as easily. They are shy or inhibited in new relationships. These potential friends need a little help in reaching out to others.

My friend Barbara specializes in cultivating friendships with the shy, quiet types. I've watched her at social gatherings. The first thing she does upon arriving is greet her old friends and briefly participate in small talk with them. Then she looks around the room for anyone who is sitting alone or who looks like she feels out of place. Barbara goes to this person and introduces herself. In no time at all she has discovered a seed of friendship. Soon they are talking and laughing together as if they were old buddies. The dormant guest no long looks uncomfortable.

Before long Barbara is introducing her new friend to her other friends, relating information about her new friend so conversation can start at a shared point of interest. Barbara always makes sure her new friend feels connected to the group before she leaves her. Days later, Barbara follows up with her new friends. As a result of reaching out to them, Barbara has added many new friends to her garden. Barbara.is a living example of what Dale Carnegie said years ago: "You can make more friends in two months by becoming interested in other people than you can in two years by trying to get other people interested in you."

I asked Barbara what motivated her to reach beyond her comfort zone to strangers when it's so much easier to visit with established friends. With sincere humility my friend answered, "It's simply a matter of putting myself in their place. I'm only doing what I would want someone else to do for me."

All of us have been in situations where we were the outsiders. We know what it feels like. When we view shy, introverted, or excluded people with empathy, sharing a few moments of friendship with them becomes more than just "doing your good deed for the day." Rather it's an opportunity to soak a dormant seed in compassion to encourage germination and growth, just as we hope others will do for us in similar situations.

Meeting new people requires patience and determination. Try to remember that you're usually not meeting the individual as she really is. You're meeting the person she wants you to think she is. Or you may meet someone who is self-conscious, defensive, and difficult to talk to because she's trying to make a good impression. Or a new acquaintance may appear to be abrupt or abrasive toward you because she's stressed out or reacting to events that happened just prior to your meeting.

Unintentional offenses like these tend to make us feel defensive and unworthy or to think this person isn't interested in us. We may fear rejection and want to back off and forget about establishing a relationship. The key is to not let any initial unpleasantness keep you from recognizing the seed of friendship that may exist in that person. Don't decide the fate of a potential friendship on your first meeting. First impressions are not always accurate.

Another reason some friendships don't germinate is because the dormant seeds are in us. There are times we don't reach out to others because we consider them spiritually, socially, or economically above us. We don't think we're interesting enough to deserve their friendship. We fail to see ourselves as God's unique and wonderful creation equipped to add new dimensions of friendship to anyone we meet. Instead, the fear of rejection keeps us trapped inside ourselves. We feel insignificant and unworthy of friendship.

All of us have faults and defects. But an unhealthy focus on your shortcomings will rob you of many enriching relationships. It only takes a few times of telling yourself "I'm not worth much" before you begin to lose sight of your worth in Christ. You end up disqualifying yourself as a valuable friend before the seed of friendship can spring to life. Sure, you should attend to areas of your life that need improvement. But don't use the fact that you are still growing as an excuse to withhold your friendship from people who may seem more mature or together than you are.

In order to look past ourselves and reach out to others, we need to establish in our hearts the reality that God loves us completely just as we are. We are God's beloved children. Jesus died to redeem us. We are complete in Him, and He is alive and active in us by His Spirit. You have every reason to be confident in reaching out to new friends. But if you fail to acknowledge God's love for you, you may find yourself sitting in the shadows feeling unworthy instead of reaching out to others who need your friendship.

A well-known speaker with a charismatic personality told me that at one time in her life she felt terribly unworthy. She had no problem addressing large crowds, but fear of rejection kept her from nurturing close friendships—and also made her very lonely.

Finally the misery of her loneliness outweighed her fear of rejection. But to change her life and reach out to others, she knew she had to do something to combat her sense of unworthiness. So every day she stood in front of her mirror and told herself, "I am a loved woman of God. God loves me." She also began searching God's Word to discover the depth of His love for her. After about 30 days she began to really believe it. With the truth of God's love as her foundation, her confidence rose, and she began extending herself to others.

Yes, overcoming your fear requires effort. When it comes to relationships, the familiar saying rings true: Nothing ventured, nothing gained. Reaching out to others means you must take the initiative. But you'll be surprised at how warmly people respond when you take the first step. Nine out of 10 times, when you initiate friendship, others will respond positively. Just be careful not to let number 10 drive you back into your defensive shell. It's by getting to know others that you will really begin to know yourself.

Okay, let's say you've done it. You've seated yourself beside a stranger and encouraged a seed of friendship to germinate by introducing yourself. Where do you go from here?

Friendships develop much like flowers do. When a seed germinates it sends down roots, sprouts leaves, and in time develops a stem and produces flowers, which contain more seeds. Similarly, friendships have four important parts.[1]

Each part is vital to the health of any relationship. As the gardener in your garden of friends, understanding how each part contributes to a friendship will help you give your friends the care they need.

Rooting a New Relationship

The first area of growth in a friendship is the root structure. Developing roots is the most important phase of a budding relationship. Roots provide stability and security for the other phases of a developing friendship.

At the root of any relationship is a combination of mutual history-giving and self-disclosure. History-giving is telling the facts and events of our lives—where we've been, what we've done, our successes and failures, etc. Self-disclosure means talking about who we are: our interests, our likes and dislikes, our relationship with Christ, etc. Notice that history-giving and self-disclosure is a process. Over time friends will disclose more of who they are and what makes them tick. Ignoring this important initial step prevents many friendships from ever beginning.

Sharing the past with family members is an important way for older and younger members to enrich the friendship basis of their relationship. I experienced this special bonding with my grandmother when she reached back into her memory to relate events of my ancestry.

She told me that she was born in Oklahoma four years before it became a state. Her parents, my great-grandparents, staked a claim with a covered wagon, two tents, a sod-walker plow, and $40. I learned that my great-grandfather was one of Daniel Boone's scouts. My great-great-grandmother was stolen by Indians at age four only to be retrieved from a squaw who lagged behind the rest of the tribe.

I was fascinated to discover my family roots. My grandmother's sharing created the foundation for a deeper friendship between us. But it never would have happened if I had not asked her to tell me about our family's background.

Mutual disclosure encourages us to trust each other as persons. That's what allows us to disclose more of our background as time goes by. When I know you understand where I'm coming from, I'm more willing to trust you to help me get where I want to go. We tend to bond with those who disclose their lives to us. Even if what a friend tells us about herself is unpleasant, our reaction is usually one of endearment rather than rejection.

But mutual disclosure is also a great risk. There's always the possibility that you may use what I tell you about myself against me. Or, once I tell you about some of my weaknesses, you may reject me. Many friendships never really get started because people are afraid to take the risk of disclosing themselves to a new friend.

Of course, we don't need to take people back to the slime pits of our past. People need to be edified by hearing the victories in our lives, not burdened down with all the dirt. There have been times when I felt led by God to reveal guarded details of my past to someone I didn't know well. Apparently they needed to hear it. But that's rare. It's okay to say, "My life was on the garbage heap at one time, but God has been faithful to change those situations in my life," without giving all the sordid details.

A practical way to facilitate history-giving and self-disclosure is to ask questions. Questions will help you focus on meaningful information with your new friend and discover common ground in your lives. Even if you and a new acquaintance do not become close friends, I guarantee that the question-and-answer process will help you both feel more comfortable the next time you are in each other's presence.

Questions and answers relating to history-giving involve sharing general information, nonthreatening facts you could share with almost anyone: where you were born and raised, the names and ages of your children, etc. Questions pertaining to self-disclosure are usually a little more personal. You would probably share this information with each other only after a certain level of trust and commitment has been established. Self-disclosure questions deal with topics such as your opinions, feelings, joys, fears, doubts, expectations, weaknesses, and strengths.

It's unrealistic to think that you can develop roots in a new friendship without discussing history-giving questions. We need to know some of this basic, objective information about each other to establish common ground. But it is equally unrealistic to expect your roots to grow deep enough to support a long-term friendship if you avoid self-disclosure questions. Friendships only really begin to develop when we get past the preliminaries to sharing something about our lives. If you and your new friend insist on keeping the dialogue on an objective level and avoid talking about what you think, how you feel, and the struggles and issues in your lives, you miss the real beauty of friendship.

Make a list of questions before you attend a social gathering or meet a new friend for coffee or lunch. Use your list of questions to guide your conversation. The process of history-giving and self-disclosure is a two-way street. You should be ready to give your answer to every question you ask your new friend.

Here are several questions you may want to include on your list. Notice that the first several are general information questions. The rest are more personal, inviting disclosure about thoughts, feelings, and personal experiences. Not all these questions are appropriate for every new acquaintance. For example, if you don't know if he or she is a Christian, you probably wouldn't ask, "How did you become a Christian?" However, there are many ways to open up a meaningful conversation.

1. Where were you born and raised?

2. How many brothers and sisters do you have? Where do they live now, and what do they do?

3. What were your favorite subjects in school?

4. How did you become a Christian?

5. Are you married? How did you meet your spouse?

6. Do you have children? What are their ages?

7. What is your happiest memory from childhood?

8. If you had your life to live over again, what would you do the same? What would you do differently?

9. What do you consider to be your greatest strengths as a person?

10. If you could ask God one question and get an immediate answer, what would it be?

11. What is the greatest joy of your life?

12. Who has been the greatest spiritual influence in your life?

13. If you unexpectedly received a $10 million inheritance, what would you do with the money?

14. What is your favorite book of the Bible? Why? Who is your favorite Bible character? Why?

15. What was your most embarrassing moment as a child? As an adult?

When you get together with a new friend, minimize the small talk and get to talking about each other as quickly as possible. I would much rather ask fairly direct questions about a new acquaintance than waste time on small talk. Surprisingly, people respond positively to this approach. I've never had anyone take offense that I wanted to know more about them. Most people are happy that someone cares enough about them to get beyond surface issues that do not address them as individuals.

The process of history-giving and self-disclosure is the first step in developing intimacy in a budding friendship. But there is much more to a plant than just roots, and there is much more to an intimate, caring friendship than just knowing about each other. In order to achieve its full flowering beauty, your friendship needs to sprout some leaves.

Drinking In the Sunshine of Affirmation

Just as the leaves of a new plant pop out of the soil in response to the warmth of the sun, a new friendship will sprout and grow in response to the warmth of affirmation. We affirm our friends when we communicate to them their value to us through loving attention and supportive, encouraging words. Plants remain dormant in the cold and dark of winter Similarly, your friendships will not spread leaves and grow without the penetrating, spring-like rays of mutual affirmation.

It is in the affirming process that acceptance is confirmed. Through history giving and self-disclosure you express to your friends that you accept their past and how it contributed to their present. Through affirmation you express that you accept them for who they are now and what they are becoming.

There is something nurturing about learning to verbalize our affirmation for our friends. But it's important that your spoken words of appreciation and encouragement are specific and personal. Instead of simply saying, "I love you," say, "I love you because..." and state a specific reason or two for your feelings. In addition to saying, "I really think you're special," describe the special qualities you're thinking about that set this friend apart from all others.

And if you don't mean it, don't say it. Words spoken merely to flatter, ingratiate, or manipulate a friend will ultimately scorch the tender leaves and wilt the friendship.

It is in the warmth of affirmation that friends are able to confront each other and encourage each other to go forward, get better, and accomplish more in every aspect of their lives. The book of Proverbs describes the result of confrontation within the context of a loving friendship: "As iron sharpens iron, so a man sharpens the countenance of his friend" (27:17, NKJV).

But our words of confrontation will only be effective when they are presented in the context of continual affirmation. Friendship should be 90 percent affirmation and only 10 percent confrontation. If we affirm our friends most of the time they will be able to receive the occasional confrontations we bring, because they know we desire the best for them and won't intentionally hurt them. We're so used to pointing out each other's faults that people tend not to believe us when we give them words of encouragement or affirmation. The abundance of spoken affirmation will assure your friends of their ongoing value to you when you must offer the sometimes painful iron-sharpening words of confrontation.

Spending Time to Grow Tall

Deep, intimate friendships grow tall and straight on the stem of fellowship. And the primary ingredients of true fellowship between friends are time and commitment.

For friendships to reach their full potential, friends must spend time together. There are a lot of instant things in the world, but friendship isn't one of them. I have taught in Bible studies that love is a four-letter word spelled T-I-M-E. The best affirmation we can offer our friends is wanting to spend time with them.

People talk a lot about "quality time" these days. There's no such thing. It's a term we invented to justify our overcrowded schedules. Fellowship requires great quantities of time, not a half-hour each month of so-called quality time. Trying to skimp on the amount of time you spend in fellowship will put a crimp in the stem of your young seedling friendship. If you spend quantity time with your friends, the quality of your fellowship will happen almost automatically.

The importance of time tells us something about how many deep friendships we can realistically maintain. If you over-seed a garden, your flowers will grow up weak and spindly due to overcrowding. By the same token, if you're involved in so many new relationships that you can't invest generous blocks of time in any of them, you may be cheating yourself and others out of meaningful friendship.

I'm not suggesting that you limit the number of your friends. After all, can you imagine announcing to a new acquaintance, "My garden of friends is full right now, but I'll be glad to take your application and get back to you as soon as there's an opening"? That's ridiculous. But you may need to be more conscious about your different friends—casual friends, close friends, intimate friends—and making sure you spend enough time with them to maintain fellowship with them.

The second key ingredient to meaningful, growth-encouraging fellowship between friends is commitment. In committing yourself to a friend, you are saying, "I care about you, I'm here for you, and I will do whatever I can to help you. You can count on me." It's a good idea to verbalize your commitment to your friends from time to time in an encouraging note or in person. But it's even more important that you live out your commitment by being the supportive nurturing friend you say you are.

Sometimes a commitment between friends is not fully reciprocal. That's how it was with my friend Nicole. For the first eight years of our friendship I honestly didn't know how she felt about me. Nicole is not one to expose her feelings—good or bad. I was committed to our friendship, but Nicole gave me the impression that she wouldn't hold me to it. I just didn't sense that she cherished or appreciated our relationship like I did. It seemed like our friendship was all one way.

When Nicole experienced some very traumatic times, I stood by her and helped her as any friend would. But from her responses I couldn't tell if she was grateful or not. I wondered if she really cared about supporting our shaky relationship. And I wondered if I should just give up and invest my time in someone else.

It was during one of Nicole's trying experiences that the Lord impressed me to make a commitment of friendship to her with no expectations for a return commitment. I knew it was primarily a commitment to be obedient and pleasing to the Lord in my relationship with Nicole. So I made the commitment before God. Sometimes a commitment to be obedient and pleasing to God helps us make the commitment to be a supportive friend.

As the years passed I lived out my commitment of friendship to Nicole time and time again. Yet I received no verbal indication of how much she cared for me. Recently that all changed. During a radio interview Nicole stated that I was one of her closest friends. I was more surprised to hear it than anyone. As a result of Nicole's revelation I was able to express to her more openly how much I care about her. Our relationship has grown since then. But it never would have happened if I hadn't obeyed God and committed myself to Nicole with no strings attached.

Self-disclosure, the process that begins at the root stage, is a vital part of strengthening the fellowship stage of a friendship. The more time friends spend together, the more they should know about each other. That doesn't mean you tell every friend everything about yourself. Self-disclosure should never exceed the level of commitment in a friendship or what people can handle. For example, you may share with an intimate friend the details of your temptations so she will pray for you and hold you accountable for purity and obedience. But you won't disclose that information to a casual friend. However, as your level of commitment to a casual friend deepens over time to that of a close friend or intimate friend, so your level of self-disclosure should deepen.

Sharing Dreams and Goals

A mature plant with sturdy roots, full leaves, and a strong stem is prepared to bloom and contribute its glorious beauty to the garden. In a friendship, the final, mature stage is the sharing of dreams and goals. Having trusted your friends with your past and your present, you are now ready to trust them with your future.

When you share your dreams with someone, you share the real you. When you start dreaming out loud in front of those you love and trust, the real you stands tall. Friends who share their dreams with each other, believe in each other, and affirm and encourage each other's dreams are truly in a position to see their friendships bloom to their fullest potential.

This is the stage at which true friends ask each other, "If you could go anywhere and do anything, knowing that God would bless you and you could not fail, what would you do?" Why? Because our dreams tell us where we want to go and often reveal God's direction for our future. And when we let our friends in on our dreams, they can help us believe for them and set goals to reach them.

Just as a flower is made up of many petals, so friends will share many dreams together. But our dreams will blow away in the wind like so many fragile petals if we don't set goals to reach them. As we share with friends our dreams concerning the spiritual, emotional, family, intellectual, physical, social, and financial areas of our lives, we need to encourage each other to set goals for seeing these dreams come true. Goals should be defined by a period of time: Where do we want to be in three months, six months, a year, five years? Mature friends will support each other, pray for each other, and hold each other accountable for the realization of their dreams.

Sowing New Seeds of Friendship

One of the greatest blessings of a mature, flowering friendship is the promise that other friendships will grow from it. It is in the flower that the seeds for the next generation of flowers are developed. Having grown through the stages of a healthy friendship, you are now prepared to germinate other healthy friendships with the people God brings into your life.

By its very nature, our garden is ever changing. It changes by hours, days, and seasons as friendships begin, develop, and mature. Some of the friends with whom we once spent a lot of time don't require as much attention. Other friends take their place for a season by requiring more attention.

Yet once a healthy friendship has developed through the four stages of history giving and self-disclosure, affirmation, fellowship, and sharing dreams and goals, it has the potential to survive a lifetime. Your garden can be blessed with such friends.

CHAPTER THREE

Finding Friends for Your Garden

For several years our friends Sam and Marty owned a vacation home on the ocean. Buying and enjoying their beach house was the fulfillment of a dream for them. In gratitude to the Lord, they committed the house to Him to be used any way He wanted.

Sam and Marty believed the Lord wanted them to use their beach house to bless their friends. They wanted it to be an expression of His love through them. So they openly made the house available as a place for friends to enjoy a nice weekend or vacation away from the city at no expense. The only request Sam and Marty made was that guests replace any supplies they used and leave the house in the same condition they found it. Unfortunately, Sam and Marty's dream of sharing their beach house with others turned into a nightmare. Many of their friends took advantage of their generosity. They didn't replace items they used or clean up after themselves. They left used sheets on the beds and dirty dishes in the sink. They left lights burning and faucets dripping. Doors were found unlocked. There were times when it looked like a hurricane had hit the beach house, a hurricane of inconsiderate behavior. Sam and Marty felt used.

The carelessness of their friends pushed Sam and Marty's commitment to the limit. After spending hours alone cleaning up after one particularly disastrous weekend, Marty screamed in disgust, "Forget it, Lord! I'm not lending this house to our friends anymore. They are rude and inconsiderate, and this whole thing stinks. If this is how they're going to thank us for the beach house, You can have them!"

After Marty's anger died down, the Lord caused her to reflect on her friendships and her commitment. "Should the way our friends treat the beach house really affect my commitment to them?" she asked herself. "Maybe they need to be taught how to love, how to think beyond themselves. What about my commitment to the Lord to be an extension of His love to my friends? Do I bail out on that just because my friends don't always live up to my expectations?"

Marty was dealing with the same basic questions we face in nurturing friendships. What's the point of relationships? What's the purpose of investing ourselves in history-giving, self-disclosure, affirmation, fellowship, and dream- and goal-sharing with others in our garden—especially when it seems to be a one-way street?

That day in the beach house Marty realized an important principle in relationships we all must grasp: *Expressing God's love in friendship is a choice to let Him bless others through us.* Sometimes it's a sacrificial choice on our part. We choose to love others whether or not they respond the way we want them to or think they should. We express God's love because we *have been blessed* by Him, not so we *can be blessed* by Him.

Whatever we receive from God is to be poured into the lives of others in our gardens, just as Jesus, our eternal Friend, has poured Himself into our lives. Jesus said, "Greater love has no one than this, that he lay down his life for his friends" (John 15:13). The apostle John added, "This is how we know what love is: Jesus Christ laid down his life for us. And we ought to lay down our lives for our brothers" (1 John 3:16). Jesus laid down His life for one reason: to reconcile people to God, that is, to bring people back into a relationship with God. That is what we are to do. Our lives should be an expression of God's love to others and should ultimately encourage our friends to develop and strengthen their relationship with God.

This is what Paul meant when he wrote that God "gave us the ministry of reconciliation" (2 Corinthians 5:18). The ultimate purpose of nurturing a healthy garden of friends is to cultivate flowers for God's beautiful bridal bouquet known as the body of Christ. For our Christian friends, that means encouraging them to grow in their commitment to Christ and their Christlike love for others. For our non-Christian friends, neighbors, and coworkers, it means sharing the gospel through loving deeds and, when God provides the opportunity, the good news about Jesus. Friendship means being in a place where our friends can experience the reality of the famous line in the musical, *Les Miserables*: "To look into the face of a friend is to see the face of God."

Ready to Love on a Moment's Notice

As caring gardeners we should continually ask God, "What do our friends need in their lives? What can we offer our friends to encourage their relationship with You?" Answering these questions may mean that we rearrange our schedules. There will be seasons when God may want us to spend more time with some friends than others. This requires us to be flexible with our friends. One of the subtle joys of nurturing a garden of friends is change.

God wants us to reach out to everyone with the same quality of love, His love. We should avoid using terms like "best friend." This kind of rating system terminology unfairly subdivides our gardens as we mentally categorize our friends into good, better, and best. Instead of looking for best friends we should be looking for the best in every person around us.

We are to show the same quality of love toward everybody—Christians and non-Christians alike, family, friends, neighbors, enemies, and strangers. Though the amount of time we commit to these different relationships may decrease as we move out from our family to the stranger, we need to be open to everyone the Lord brings into our lives. Perhaps the needs of some will require special attention. Our gardens should be a haven of love in an impersonal world. Many times the friendship of unconditional love will require sacrificing our time, talent, and resources. Regardless of whether or not we enjoy it, God has called us to extend His love to everyone.

We are to "be prepared in season and out of season" (2 Timothy 4:2) when it comes to extending ourselves to others in love. We never know when God might want to use our loving friendship to edify a Christian or reach out to a non-Christian.

My husband Rich implements this principle in his accounting business, although accountants are often thought to be more numbers-oriented than people-oriented. Even when Rich goes into a meeting to discuss financial matters, he is open to the Holy Spirit's intervention at any moment with anyone who walks in his door. This policy has led to some rather interesting experiences.

One such experience occurred not too long ago. An attractive couple came to Rich's office to divvy up their finances and property before going to divorce court. But as they were talking to Rich about their estate, the Holy Spirit was talking to him about their relationship. The insights and prompting Rich was receiving made him groan inside, "Lord, you've got to be kidding. Why me?"

Finally, with a loving yet firm approach, Rich began to talk to his clients about their relationship. Rich's insight revealed to the husband his feelings of resentment toward his wife, which had opened the door to an extramarital affair. At this point Rich appeared to be the man's enemy. He wanted to punch my husband for revealing his secret to his wife. By this time his wife was bawling buckets of tears, causing Rich's coworkers in adjacent offices to wonder how bad the couple's financial situation could be!

This story has a happy ending, however, which was actually a happy beginning for this couple. Both husband and wife have come to the Lord, and together they are seeking to restore their marriage through counseling. How did it come about? Because one man, who was tuned in to the opportunities around him to extend love, rolled up his sleeves and became a friend to two clients with great needs.

We are presented with opportunities like this nearly every day. I'm not saying that you will lead every stranger you meet to the Lord. But if you live each day committed to being an extension of God's love, you will be a useful instrument of love, reconciliation, and friendship in His hands to Christians and non-Christians alike.

"Special Delivery" Friends

Sometimes God allows us to take a less bold, more gradual approach to pointing people to Him. These are the people the Master Florist will special deliver to our doorstep. They are often our neighbors and long-term friends or acquaintances. We have plenty of time to transplant them into our gardens and cultivate their friendships. It is very important, however, for us not to become complacent about loving these people. We need to be ever mindful of directing them toward God without judging whether or not they have the potential of being part of God's beautiful bouquet.

Fifteen years ago the house next to ours was up for sale. Finding a buyer was going to take a major miracle, because the house reeked to high heaven. The former tenants had two huge dogs that ran the place, including using the ghastly, bright blue carpet as a bathroom.

When I saw the "sold" sticker on the real estate sign, my first inclination was, "What kind of people would buy a house in such bad shape?" My fears were dispelled when one day the smelly blue carpet was piled in a heap on the curb, and rolls of neutral-colored carpet were installed. Before we even met our new neighbors I thought, "They must be alright; they hate the blue carpet as much as I did." I was hopeful that a good relationship would develop.

Paula and her husband, our new neighbors, were sweet, enjoyable people. But Rich and I soon discovered we could not immediately share with them the most important part of our lives: our relationship with Jesus. Both of them had negative church experiences in their background. Neither of them understood the personal aspect of a relationship with God.

The Lord revealed to me that these neighbors would only come to Him after watching our lifestyle Nothing Rich and I could say would have a lasting effect on either Paula or her husband. So our relationship was established on the common ground of raising children and sharing the routine chores of life. Our loyalty and respect for each other as neighbors grew through the years.

Eventually we realized that our dear friends had large cracks in their marriage. As Paula's trust in our friendship grew and the pain in her marriage increased, she began to ask why our marriage seemed so firmly founded. Finally, the door was open to speak. In the midst of her pain, Paula accepted Jesus as her Lord.

My 15-year friendship with Paula is the result of an investment of time. I invested the time, and God gave me Paula's friendship. Ralph Waldo Emerson once wrote, "I didn't find my friends; the good God gave them to me." I feel privileged that God special-delivered Paula to me and entrusted her to my garden. She has truly been a gift to me.

You may be tempted to think that your long-term investment of time and friendship in neighbors or friends is fruitless. Be encouraged. Continue to share yourself with them, affirm them, fellowship with them, and share dreams and goals at the appropriate level. God is using your loving commitment to them to reveal Himself. Your friendship is making a difference in their lives.

Friends on the Close-out Table

A fabulous place to find new friends is on the close-out tables of life. These people have been beaten up by circumstances and are ready to give up on others. Their personal lives are in shambles. Their marriages are falling apart. Their children are out of control. Their businesses are failing. Like potted flowers on the close-out table at the nursery, they are drooping and their leaves are turning yellow, believing God has overlooked their dark circumstances. They attend meetings where Christians are gathered, desperately hoping for answers and for positive relationships. They feel cheap or worthless.

We often think twice before investing our time in cultivating a friendship with these people. We're not sure the benefits will be worth the effort. Even if these friends take root and grow in our garden, it may take a lot of time and effort to help them overcome the effects of what they've been through. They're not exactly going to look terrific in our garden for a while. We're afraid to get involved rescuing these delicate treasures for God, afraid we'll get dirty.

So what do these friends with little or no hope have to offer anyway? They simply offer us a chance to be an expression of God's love. These people need tender loving care. They long for someone to value them and love them as people, to give them a taste of God's love and a hope for the future.

When Al first came to my friend Barbara's home fellowship group he was quite a loner. Barbara wasn't sure if Al didn't know how to talk to people or just didn't want to. And others in the group didn't feel comfortable striking up a conversation with Al. His appearance was very intimidating. His long, dark brown hair framed a stern face.

But Barbara decided that Al's appearance and withdrawn behavior weren't going to keep her from being a friend to Al. She saw an opportunity to be an expression of God's love to a hurting human being.

But it wasn't easy being Al's friend. Most of the time he limited his responses to "yeah" or "no." So instead of allowing her relationship with Al to remain on a superficial level, my friend began to pray for him in order to understand him better. The Holy Spirit helped her come up with a better way to express God's love to Al.

During the following months, Barbara asked Al insightful questions without making Al feel like she was infringing upon his private life. Actually, Al desperately wanted someone to care. But he needed to know someone really wanted to hear what he had to say and how he truly felt. Barbara became that person. She nurtured him with love and hope, and Al's faith began to grow.

Al became a true friend of Barbara and her husband, actually living in their home for several years. During that time their relationship was mutually rewarding. They learned so much from each other. Al taught his new friends the importance of silence, of just sitting and thinking about things. And they helped Al overcome his fear of people, see the value of his identity in Christ, and boldly express himself to others.

Some of the most precious friends God has given me are those who desperately needed a friend. If He had not pointed them out, I probably would have never been drawn to them. As you extend God's love freely to others, you may have the same experience. Some of these people need only a temporary friendship, moving out of your life as soon as their wounds heal. But others may stay the rest of your life. Regardless, we need to be sensitive enough to plant these friends in our window boxes. There they can temporarily live under our watchful eye and receive the daily nurturing of God's love. We won't have all the answers concerning their painful circumstances, but we can assure them God does. And those answers come when we take time to pray with them and encourage them in God's Word.

We must be very careful not to take credit for the healing our hurting friends experience through God's love. Sometimes a subtle pride arises when God uses us to rescue someone from life's close-out table. We look at our comforted friend and say to ourselves, "Wow, I really did that right; I'm a great friend!" In reality, we are merely an extension of God's love, and we must direct all the praise to Him.

Our Wild Bunch of Family Friends

There is another category of people we sometimes neglect touching for God with friendship: our families. We sometimes see family members as a strange assortment of flowers resembling weeds. We classify them as "the wild bunch" and question from time to time if they are truly our friends at all.

As with other friends in our garden, appreciating our families is a matter of perspective. We need to make sure we see them through God's eyes and treat them with the same tenderness and respect we give our other friends. If we take time to notice them as individuals, we discover the beauty of this patch of wild flowers in our gardens. I have a friend who keeps a written record of when and how often she visits, calls, or writes each of her family members. This method helps her touch her family with God's love more consistently.

But instead of looking for ways to be an expression of God's love to our families, sometimes we avoid them. Of all the flowers in our garden, family members often irritate us the most. Members of our family have a way of exposing our weaknesses. So we conveniently move across town or across the continent, limiting our interaction with these "wild flowers" to holidays or special family gatherings. And even when we do get together, we spray our relatives with poisonous words of jealousy or trample them with sarcastic remarks. We don't think twice about these unloving expressions, assuming it's normal family behavior. We fail to see family members as those to whom we should be extending God's love and our friendship.

In reality, our relatives should be the foremost recipients of our loving friendship. We must view them as people God has brought into our lives for us to love. Instead of treating them like the wild bunch, we must seek to cultivate them in our garden with the same care we devote to our most treasured friends.

If you find it difficult to extend unconditional love and friendship to certain family members, the reason may be rooted in your past family relationships.

God can heal these hurts if you seek His wisdom and invite His love to flow through you in fullness to family members.

Within the larger circle of parents, brothers and sisters, aunts and uncles, grandparents, and cousins is a special group of family members. Because of your unique relationship under God to this small group of people, your first energies of love and friendship belong to them. They are the members of your immediate family: your husband and children. Your friendship with this special circle of friends in your garden deserves a closer look.

CHAPTER FOUR

The Special Circle of Friends in Your Garden

Many of the friends who flourish in your garden today will be your friends for years to come. If you're really blessed, some of the flowers you nurture in your garden will be around for decades, and a few will endure a lifetime. But there is only one friendship that has been ordained by God to remain "till death do us part." If you are married, you made such a vow of love and commitment on your wedding day. You have one special friend in the center of your garden of friends who must be cherished above all others: your husband.

For many of us, the intimate, loving circle of friendship in marriage has expanded to include the children God has blessed us with. To them also we reserve the highest level of devotion in friendship. Other friends may come and go, but our commitment of unconditional love must find its highest priority in our relationship with our husbands and children.

If there is any place where the four stages of friendship—self-disclosure, affirmation, fellowship, and dream- and goal-sharing—are being perfected, it should be between husband and wife and between parents and children. If there is any place where the love described in 1 Corinthians 13:4-7 is lovingly exercised, it should be within the family. The home should be the primary and daily proving ground for the patience, kindness, encouragement, humility, selflessness, forgiveness, truth, protection, faith, hope, and perseverance of unconditional love. Your husband and your children can be your forever friends in the truest sense of the word.

A Difference of Perspective

The first thing to understand in nurturing a friendship with your husband (and other special men in your life, such as brothers, brothers-in-law, and husbands of your close women friends) is that men perceive friendship differently than women. For example, when you ask the average man, "How would you describe the ideal friend?" he will likely respond, "Someone I can enjoy doing something with" whereas a woman will answer the same question, "Someone I can talk to about anything."

These responses reveal the first difference in how men and women approach friendship. Women are basically relationship-oriented. Men are basically task-oriented. They direct much of their energy to work, hobbies, sports, creating, building, and fixing. When they can perform these tasks with other men and gain a sense of accomplishment or affirmation, they experience a satisfying level of friendship.

Men enjoy great camaraderie playing golf, watching a basketball game, or rebuilding an engine together. But without tasks to get involved in or talk about together, many men find meaningful relationships difficult to maintain. As a result, men often find their gardens looking more like vacant lots where only a few volunteers grow.

In many cases a man's wife may be the only person with whom he actively seeks to establish a real friendship. Many men believe a close relationship with their wife is the only one they need. Based on a review of over 200 studies on gender and intimacy, men "report being less close than women are to friends and . . . more likely than women to name spouse or sweetheart as best friend."[1]

The second significant difference between men and women impacting our respective approaches to friendship involves emotions. Women tend to be emotionally expressive, while men tend to be emotionally repressive. *USA Today* reported, "Men still stay at a greater emotional distance from others than do women, and they pay for this detachment with poorer health, more loneliness and problems related to their children, psychologists say." Quoting psychologist Ronald Levant of the Harvard Medical School, the article continues, "Although biological differences may explain part of the intimacy gap, 'the lion's share is due to socialization,' Levant says. Male infants are more emotionally expressive, but boys are taught to stifle emotions—particularly uncomfortable ones like fear, sadness and shame—while girls are allowed freer rein."[2]

From their youth, men have been taught, "Big boys don't cry." They grow up developing a false image of toughness. After years of wearing this macho mask, men start to believe the image. The sensitive, emotionally expressive person God created them to be is locked behind the external shell of toughness ingrained in them since childhood.

My friend Dan noticed this tough-versus-tender emphasis several years ago when he was saying good-bye to a good friend and his family. Dan bent over to give his friend's seven-year-old son a kiss on the cheek. The boy informed him, "Men don't kiss children." Feeling a bit awkward, Dan decided just to hug the boy. "Men don't hug either," the boy said, then turned to his father, "do they Dad?" Dan's friend shook his head, confirming his son's belief. The boy turned to Dan and extended his hand for a handshake.

The episode almost broke Dan's heart. That day he decided to show his friend how important it is for men to express their emotions to each other. Every time he saw his friend thereafter he made it a point to hug him and tell him how much he loved and appreciated him. Dan's expressions made his friend uncomfortable at first. But eventually the man finally learned to respond to Dan by hugging him in return and verbalizing his love. Unfortunately, emotional expression of any kind is rather rare among most men.

A third difference between men and women that impacts friendship is that women are more disposed to vulnerability and intimacy in relationships while men are more competitive. Being task-oriented, men need to display strength, solve problems, compete, and win in their work and play. Therefore they tend to be tough tiger lilies in their relationships, particularly with other men.

One of the most insightful conversations I've ever had on the subject of friendship from a male perspective was on a plane trip. The man sitting next to me was returning home after visiting two of his old college fraternity buddies. The three of them had a lot in common when they were in school: similar family backgrounds, scholarships, and addiction to football. Now in their mid-forties, the three men maintain a very close relationship, getting together twice a year.

But when all three of them get together, they don't discuss anything from their hearts. Only when they are together one on one do they share at that depth. Even though they all end up knowing the same information about each other, their competitive nature won't allow them to open up when they are all together. Their experience is typical of how many men approach intimacy in relationships.

As a result of all these differences, women tend to be more adept at communication than men. Men often have only a partial understanding of true communication. When I asked three male flowers in my garden to define communication, they gave me three different answers which together represent a balanced concept of what it means to communicate.

Dan thinks of communication as the ability to openly discuss any topic. To him, communication means being vulnerable to a friend, discussing the bad along with the good.

Buddy believes communication has more to do with what we hear than what we say. To him, perception and understanding of what is being communicated is everything. Disagreements and misunderstanding occur in relationships because people perceive messages differently than they are intended.

My husband Rich's definition focuses on all the non-verbal aspects of communicating. Effective communication involves sending messages through our actions as well as our words.

Don't be surprised if you are better than your husband overall at communication in your relationship. After all, his upbringing has likely centered his attention on what he does and how well he succeeds than on how he relates to others. He may have been coached from an early age to keep his thoughts and feelings to himself and only show his strengths. This is not to say that husbands can't communicate but that women generally have a head start on this skill. Your husband's possible disadvantage in this area will impact how he deals with the four stages of friendship in your relationship.

Nurturing a Friendship with the Main Man in Your Garden

All these male-female differences, plus the resulting limitations in communication men often experience, don't in any way disqualify men from being good friends. But they do present some unique challenges to the wife who desires to develop a nurturing friendship with the main man in her garden.

Because of the nature of your commitment, you and your husband should enjoy the deepest level of involvement at all four stages of your friendship—self-disclosure, affirmation, fellowship, and dream/goal sharing. But it doesn't always work out that way. Even your husband's claim that you are his best or only friend is no guarantee he is ready to participate in the stages of friendship at the level you are. Actually, many of the masculine traits he brings into the relationship may hinder him from being the kind of friend you hope for.

The key to nurturing your friendship with this most-prized flower in your garden is understanding his differences and being sensitive to them in your expressions of friendship. You can't nag him, bribe him, or cajole him into being a better friend. But your patient, loving attention to being his friend will free him to grow in his friendship toward you.

Your husband's tendency to be task-oriented, emotionally repressive, competitive, and less communicative may inhibit him at the history-giving and self-disclosure stage of friendship. For example, when he arrives home from work he may not want to talk much about his day, especially if he doesn't feel like he accomplished much or has experienced a failure. It will probably be easier for him to discuss what he has done than what he thinks or how he feels.

To make him feel at ease at this stage, ask him about his work, how his day went, if he met anyone interesting, and share with him something about the tasks you're involved in. But also encourage him to greater self-disclosure by sharing your thoughts, opinions, and feelings about things in your life together. Invite him to share who he is apart from what he does by asking him, "What do you think about...?" or "How do you feel about...?"

The affirmation stage of friendship is a problem for men who are strongly task-oriented and competitive. Such men may find it difficult to communicate affirmation and acceptance to others, including their wives, if they can't see how it will help them achieve, conquer, or gain some kind of personal advantage.

The best way for you to help your husband grow as an affirmer in your relationship is to model affirmation with no ulterior motives. Describe to him often the character qualities as well as the physical qualities you appreciate in him. When you tell him you love him, also tell him why. And never use affirmation as a tool to try to persuade him to do something or buy something for you. That's not affirmation; it's manipulation. The more he feels affirmed and appreciated just for who he is, the easier it will be for him to remove his competitive armor and affirm you.

The fellowship stage of a friendship requires time spent together developing intimacy. This is sometimes a problem for the wife whose task-oriented, competitive husband always has to be doing something to feel fulfilled. He puts in long hours on the job only to come home and spend the evening puttering in his shop, playing basketball with the guys, or watching his favorite team on TV. How can you encourage fellowship and develop intimacy when you're only alone together a few minutes a day?

Perhaps the best place to start is to plan to be with him as often as possible while he's doing whatever he's doing. For example, if he likes to work in his shop in the evening, find an area of the shop you can occupy and work on your own hobby. If he likes to attend sporting events, do as one woman does: Attend with him occasionally and take a book along. You can talk between innings or during halftime and time-outs. When it's possible and appropriate, accompany him on business trips. And always be prepared with questions and topics that will encourage (not badger!) him to talk with you when he can.

Even in the intimacy and trust experienced in marriage, many men struggle with the fourth stage of friendship: dream- and goal-sharing. Often when a wife begins to share her dreams for the future with her husband, as the task-oriented family provider, he feels obligated to fulfill them for her. If the dreams are too lofty for him to fulfill, he will try to discourage her so he won't feel like a failure. As a result, she will stop communicating her dreams, and then even realistic, achievable dreams and goals will not be shared. And when dreams and goals are not shared, the friendship will not blossom to its full potential.

When two people greatly value each other, they will help set goals and dream dreams for each other, because they see great potential in each other. If Rich hadn't maintained his dream of me writing this book and hadn't encouraged me to set goals for its completion, it never would have happened. He valued me and this project more than I did. He truly showed himself to be my friend by helping me reach my potential in this area. The same thing can happen in your relationship as you dream achievable dreams and set realistic goals for each other, then together enjoy seeing your friendship grow and blossom.

Working Together Toward Intimacy

Since intimate friendship comes more naturally to women, you may sometimes feel like you carry the responsibility for initiating all the emotionally close times between you and your husband. Nothing could be further from what God has in mind for marriage. Ideally, each partner is working to nurture the relationship and initiate times of sharing and fellowship. The husband is to regard his wife as his own body and be as sensitive to her needs as to his own (Ephesians 4:25-28). The wife is to regard her husband with respect and surrender to his leadership in the home (vv. 22-24). In this deepest of all human relationships, God calls us to love sacrificially and unconditionally, to put our partner's needs above our own.

However, in the area of building intimacy in the day-to-day life of marriage, you may need to show the way with great patience and love in order for the flower of marital friendship to bloom and flourish in your marriage. Sensitivity and emotional vulnerability, which come more easily for a woman, are gifts you can bring to the marriage friendship to fulfill both your husband and yourself.

How can women encourage their husband toward this highest level of mutual friendship? If you are starting at the beginning in this area of friendship with your husband, you may suggest to him that you would like to participate with him in one of his activities so you can share his enjoyment in the event (even though it may not be one that you naturally enjoy). By doing this you demonstrate your willingness to get to know him on another level and share in his interests.

Likewise, you can ask him to share in something you enjoy and that is emotionally satisfying to you. This may require your husband to step outside his comfort zone, and you will probably meet with some resistance. Don't be discouraged or feel that your interests are not as worthwhile as his. Sharing an afternoon of shopping, with a break for coffee, may not be your husband's idea of enjoying a Saturday afternoon. But if you have agreed to explore each other's areas of interest, this is one way he can love you as he loves himself.

Wives often feel they are the ones who must continually make the effort to engage their husbands in meaningful conversation and shared times of fun and fellowship. To balance this out, one wife I know asks her husband to suggest 10 things he would like to do or places he would like to go during the year, and she does the same. Throughout the year they find creative ways to spend time together doing these various activities. Another way to get your husband involved in something with you is to suggest an activity neither of you have attempted before.

In order for any relationship to flourish, there must be mutual respect. Learning how you can respect your husband's unique needs while communicating your own is the challenge of building true unity in marriage.

Ultimately, your husband must take responsibility for shifting his more natural task-orientation toward a more relational one. You should never feel you must overcompensate for what he may lack in his abilities and skills to develop a closer friendship with you. You can and should encourage him, but you must never demand or force change. It must be his choice to develop his relationships. And what applies to women applies also to men: A close friendship, whether with a spouse or anyone else, is best established by following God's guidelines.

One final thought about friendship and the special man in your life. Don't overlook the significance of encouraging your husband's friendships with other men, especially where self-disclosure, affirmation, fellowship, and dream- and goal-sharing are practiced. He needs friends he can relate to beyond activities. His growth as a nurturing friend with other men will enrich his friendship with you.

Being a Friend to Your Children

Like your husband, your children occupy a special place in your garden reserved for the most important of all your relationships. While your friendship with your husband should continue to grow steady and strong "till death do us part," your relationship with your children will go through some marked changes over the years.

Childhood is the phase of dependence. Your children come into the world utterly dependent upon you. They regard you as the most important person in their lives. You are parent, provider, protector, counselor, and guide. Your children may enjoy many other friendships during childhood, but in this phase no other adult or peer loves them and cares for them the way you do.

Adolescence is the phase of transition. Your children are still dependent on you for meeting many of their basic needs, but they are discovering their potential for independence. You are gradually being eased out of the spotlight as they develop significant relationships with their peers, especially those of the opposite sex.

Adulthood is the phase of independence. Your children are still your children, but their friendship with you takes on a new dimension based on whom (or if) they choose to marry, where they choose to live, and what they choose to do with their lives. Yours is no longer the most important relationship in their lives.

But until they reach this third phase, you have a tremendous opportunity to cultivate a foundation for a healthy friendship with your children and help prepare them for growing a garden of friends of their own. While your children are quite young, you will take most of the initiative in self-disclosure, affirmation, fellowship, and dream- and goal-sharing. But because your children are experts at imitation, they will eventually learn these skills of friendship-nurturing through your example and begin to practice them in their relationships with you and with others. The following ideas will help you nurture the four stages of a friendship with your children while they are still under your roof.

Encourage history-giving and self-disclosure with your children by talking to them about everything, even before they are old enough to carry on a conversation with you. Statements like, "I feel happy because...," "I love Daddy because...," "I love Jesus because...," etc. will assure them at an early age that it's OK to talk about our thoughts and feelings. Talk about what you did during their nap or while they were visiting Grandma. This will pave the way for them to feel comfortable sharing what they did at school and with their friends. Your willing self-disclosure about activities, thoughts, and feelings will help keep communication lines open as they grow older.

As they grow, begin to relate to them your family history with positive, uplifting stories that are appropriate to their age and understanding. Talk about your parents and grandparents. Relate your own personal history—how you met your husband, how you became a Christian, significant turning points in your walk with the Lord and your personal growth. Your openness in history-giving will encourage them to anticipate growth and change in their own lives.

There are many ways to nurture friendship with our children through affirmation. One of the most important is by developing mutual respect in the family. Respect is an important equalizer, and friendship happens best between equals.

Respect means parents give children room to change and grow, and children give parents room to change and grow. Respect means talking in the same civil tone with our children as we do with our closest friends. Respect means never complaining to our friends about our children behind their backs. Respect means never intentionally embarrassing our children in front of other people. Respect means not forcing our friends on our children, yet being open to encourage and share in their friendships.

Respect also means getting down to your children's level sometimes and having fun. Our friends Jimmy and Carol Owens always had a lot of fun with their children Buddy and Jamie and their friends. One night after the family had gone to bed, Jimmy and Carol heard something outside. They peeked out and discovered that four of Buddy and Jamie's friends were getting ready to cover the yard with toilet paper.

Our two adult friends snuck onto the front porch, crouched behind some shrubs, and picked up the garden hose. Just as the four young people began to play their prank, Jimmy and Carol played one of their own. They let the teenagers have it with a cold blast of water, sending them screaming and squealing with laughter down the street. Jimmy and Carol had as much fun as their four wet "victims." And they also enjoyed the respect of their two children for their spontaneity and willingness to have fun.

The affirmation stage of friendship includes confrontation, and confronting children often involves correction. Christian marriage and family counselor H. Norman Wright explains that even correction should be done in a positive manner: "Corrective messages must be delivered in a positive, affirmative way. We don't correct our children to make them feel bad, but to help them discover a better way to do something. . . . Share your messages of correction in a tone of voice that reflects your care and concern. Our tone has five times the impact of our words."[3]

Positive correction is another way of showing respect for your children. For every scold make sure they get 10 praises. Tell them 10 ways they are special to you or 10 things they are doing right. Give them the overall impression that you are pleased with their behavior except for a few things which must be corrected, instead of making them think that most everything they do is wrong.

Another way to affirm and respect our children as they grow older is to encourage their independence by allowing them to negotiate with you. When our daughter Amy turned 14, she decided that some of our rules and regulations were too strict. One evening she met privately with Rich and I and presented her written requests. It read: "Now that I am 14, I think I should be able to: (1) Go to the mall by myself with my friends; (2) Choose whatever movies I want to see; (3) Go to the movies by myself with my friends; (4) Decide on my own bedtime; (5) Wear whatever clothes I want to wear, including swimsuits; (6) Listen to whatever music I want," and the list continued.

After reading her list, Amy concluded, "Well, what do you think?" We assured her that we respected the way she came to us with her concerns because it showed she was growing and maturing. We told her that it hadn't been so long ago that we were having the same conversation with our parents. We promised to pray about and discuss her requests and get back to her in a couple of days. Rich and I felt God had given us the original guidelines, so we needed to ask Him what changes we needed to make at this stage of Amy's maturing process.

After a few days we sat down with Amy and went over her list point by point. We gave our reasons why we could or could not grant each request. As a result of the negotiating, Amy's bedtime was extended. We also said she could wear whatever she wanted, providing it was modest. She gained some of her freedoms while others would have to wait for greater levels of maturity.

We asked her how she felt about our decisions. Amy said, "I feel good. It's alright." She realized that Rich and I had heard and understood her and taken her concerns to the Lord. She felt affirmed, and our relationship with her was strengthened through the entire process.

The third stage of friendship, fellowship, requires that we spend time with our children to develop intimacy in our relationship. And since friendship within the family is a high priority, time with children must be reserved on the calendar and carefully kept. This means arranging schedules to attend our childrens' school and outside activities as often as possible. It means being together as often as possible at mealtimes and bedtimes. It means planning family evenings at home, outings, and vacations. Remember: There is no "quality time" with your children that can compensate if you neglect for spending quantities of time with them.

Time spent communicating with our children is an important part of developing a lasting friendship with them. Open lines of communication help prevent misunderstandings from occurring between parent and child.

My friend Irene became aware of how a lack of communication can spark problems in a parent-child friendship. Irene and her husband had to move to a small retirement community with their young son Tim. Being pregnant with her second child, she expressed a concern to her husband about finding a rental that welcomed children in an adult-oriented community.

Every day Irene and Tim drove through the community following up ads for rentals. Her main question to the landlords was, "Do you accept children?" Day after day they answered no. As the days went by and the rejections continued, Tim's behavior got worse and worse. He had always been his mother's little buddy, but his behavior was showing a lack of respect.

Finally my nerve-frayed friend confronted her son. "Why are you acting this way? What's wrong with you?"

With tears streaming down his face the little boy replied, "Why don't you want me anymore? Every day you ask a bunch of people if they accept children. Just 'cause you're having a new baby you're trying to give me away, and nobody else wants me either."

Irene had no idea Tim was misinterpreting her actions as a message of rejection. She quickly realized how more openness in communication could have prevented a needless and painful misunderstanding for Tim.

Fellowship in building a friendship with our children also requires commitment. Our children must know that we are totally committed to them now and in the future. Gary Smalley writes:

> Norma and I frequently tell our children that we love them. In many ways, we let them know that we are committed to them for their entire lives, no matter what they do. We are committed to help them be successful in whatever they want to do. We are committed to them after they are married.... We will be

committed to their mates and to their children. We tell them we are always available to listen. Should they get into trouble, we will be there to help....They know how much we love them and that nothing can ever keep us from loving them.[4]

The time and commitment you share with your children will help build a rich friendship.

The final stage of friendship is dream- and goal-sharing. At this stage in our friendship with our children we must lay the foundation for them to believe their dreams can come true and to guide them in setting their goals accordingly. This requires that we invite them to tell us about their dreams by playing games like "What if...?" or "What would I be if...?"

Open-ended questions like these will encourage them to verbalize what they want to do, try, or be in the future.

Part of laying the foundation for achieving their dreams and goals is our responsibility to cultivate their talents and supply the education that will make their dreams a reality. Sometimes they may not see the importance of establishing the groundwork for their dreams through such "boring" things as school and lessons. They may not be mature or responsible enough to choose what they need to do to see their dreams come true. This is where our experience and perspective can help prepare them for fulfillment in the future.

An important part of this stage is to honor each child's uniqueness instead of pressing them into the precise mold we have for their lives. How do you honor a child's uniqueness? Take time to watch and listen to each one of them. Spend time having fun together. Discover how interesting they are and how different they are from each other. Allow each one to blossom as an individual—each with his own needs, likes, and dreams—instead of lumping them together and making them conform to your idea of what they should be. Learn what methods are best for teaching each one to become independent from you and dependent on God. Rarely is the same method effective for every child in a family.

We must make sure our children are not limited in their dreams and goals by our experiences or expectations. Sometimes we try to develop our children into the kind of people we want them to be. Norm Wright explains, "We all have a tendency to mold our children to match the design we have for their lives. If their unique tendencies threaten us, we try to make these differences disappear. Basically, we are comfortable with others who are like us. Thus we unwittingly attempt to fashion our children into a revised edition of ourselves. We want them to be created in our image. But that puts us in conflict with God who wants them to be created in His image."[5]

Oftentimes when we label a child, even positively with words like "extrovert" or "athletic," we are sending a message of our expectations. Labeling can prevent a child's uniqueness from blossoming. Within the context of general guidance and helpfulness, we must be careful not to impose our dreams or goals on our children. We are responsible to God to train and teach our children to grow into God's image and follow His dreams and goals for their lives. He has given us the task of helping our children learn to develop close, emotionally satisfying relationships.

Prior to the twentieth century, most families in our country lived in a rural setting separated from other families by acres of farmland. Individual families worked together, learned together, and played together. Children grew up with parents who were their primary educators, employers, and friends. The family was the closest of all relationships.

Today the family is under the pressure of modern society. Most fathers and many mothers spend several hours a day working away from the home. Children are shuffled off to baby sitters, day care, preschool, and school where they are compartmentalized by age away from their siblings. Evenings and weekends are filled with church activities, music lessons, clubs, and sports, often sending dad, mom, and the kids in different directions.

In the old days, nurturing a healthy garden of family friends was easy because the family was together most of the time. Today friendship between husband and wife and between parents and children is far from automatic. If it's going to happen, we must make it happen. But by carefully and consistently applying the attributes of unconditional love through the stages of friendship with those who make up this special circle in your life, you will find that your husband and children will be among your nearest and dearest forever friends.

CHAPTER FIVE

A Bouquet for the Friend of Friends

South of Amsterdam in the Netherlands near Schiphol Airport is the lakeside community of Aalsmeer, home of the celebrated Aalsmeer Flower Auction—*Centrale Aalsmeerse Bloemenveiling*—the largest of 12 cut-flower auctions in Holland. The Aalsmeer auction takes place in the world's largest commercial building, covering an area equal to 60 football fields.

Five days a week, from well before dawn until just before noon, the parking lot bustles with truckloads of carefully packed flowers. Dendrobium orchids are flown in from Thailand. Anemones come from Israel. Tuberoses arrive from Mexico. Trucks and barges transport cyclamens from within Holland. Cut flowers are assembled at the auction to be purchased and shipped elsewhere to fulfill their destiny.

Inside, approximately 4000 registered buyers do business with an equal number of registered growers. Buyers must know quality when they see it. Bidding takes place at the rate of 600 final bids per hour, and only one bid is accepted per lot of flowers. In a typical day an average of nine million cut flowers change hands. Only 12-48 hours elapse from the time these delicate flowers are cut until they are for sale in flower shops around the world.

Like the flowers purchased at the Aalsmeer Flower Auction, each of us in the body of Christ has been selected and has a destiny to fulfill. We're like a bouquet of flowers gathered by the Master Florist for Him to enjoy and share with the world. Paul wrote, "God . . . reconciled us to himself through Christ and gave us the ministry of reconciliation: that God was reconciling the world to himself in Christ, not counting men's sins against them. And he has committed to us the message of reconciliation" (2 Corinthians 5:18,19). The Greek word for reconcile is *katallasso*. It means "to change from enmity to friendship."[1]

It's only by being a friend of God that we are able to reach out in love to nurture the friends He brings to our gardens.

Growing as God's Friends

But how do we become God's friends after having been His enemies through sin? Developing an intimate friendship with God follows the same four stages any other close friendship follows, except it's on a somewhat grander scale.

First, there must be history-giving and self-disclosure. God reveals Himself to us in the Old and New Testaments. We see what He's like and how He loved and redeemed people who didn't love Him. The more we understand from the Bible who God is and what He's done, the more we're willing to trust Him and risk our side of self-disclosure: confession and repentance. We share our background with Him by admitting that our roots were in the world. Just as the flowers of Aalsmeer must be cut from their roots to begin their journey toward their intended destiny, so we must cut our ties to our old ways. Only then can we be picked for the Master's use.

Second, intimate friendship with God continues with affirmation. At this stage our value to God is acknowledged. The value of the flowers at the Aalsmeer auction is an estimated $3 billion annually. The value of a flower or anything else is determined by the price someone is willing to pay for it. Your value was set at the cross with only one bid: the blood of Jesus. The Master Florist paid the ultimate price for you. It was the only bid God would accept. In return, your affirmation is to open your life to Jesus and receive His generous provision of forgiveness.

In friendship we both affirm others and confront the issues in their lives.

At Bethlehem Jesus affirmed us by taking on our humanity; at Calvary He confronted the main issue in our lives by dying on the cross for our sin. God continues to affirm us and confront us every day through His Word, the Holy Spirit, and our loving, affirming friends.

Third, God cultivates intimate friendship with us through fellowship, spending time with us. He doesn't just spend *some* time with us; He's with us all the time. Jesus loves us enough to say, "I am with you always, to the very end of the age" (Matthew 28:20). He is present with us constantly through the Holy Spirit (John 14:16-18).

As flowers in the body of Christ, we find ourselves arranged in a vase called the kingdom of God. It is there we develop intimacy in fellowship with God by spending time with Him. Our part in fellowship requires drinking in the Holy Spirit, reading God's Word, communicating with Him, worshiping Him for who He is, praising Him for what He's done, asking Him through prayer to meet our needs and desires, and letting Him reveal to us how He would like to express His love through us to our friends. It is at the fellowship level of friendship that our motivation changes. Our main desire is no longer "God, what can You do for me?" but "God, what can I do for you?"

Fourth, intimate friendship with God progresses to the final stage of intimacy: sharing goals and dreams. God's love for us is seen in the incredible goals and dreams He has for us now and in eternity. At the end of His earthly ministry Jesus revealed His eternal plan for us: "In my Father's house are many rooms; if it were not so, I would have told you. I am going there to prepare a place for you. And if I go and prepare a place for you, I will come back and take you to be with me that you also may be where I am" (John 14:2,3).

The Master Florist is returning for the body of Christ, a bride "without stain or wrinkle or any other blemish, but holy and blameless" (Ephesians 5:27). He will not accept any crimped stems, discolored petals, or yellowing leaves in His bridal bouquet. His flowers must eloquently communicate a message of deepest devotion. We are designed for perfection and arranged with an eye for eternity.

For us to dream with God, we must develop an eye for eternity. We must become eternity-minded. Because Jesus has promised us a glorious eternal future with Him, we are able to work hard and suffer long serving Him and others now. At this depth of friendship with God we can accept the different trials and testings in life with joy, because our focus—our dreams and plans—are based on eternal, not temporal, values and rewards (James 1:2-4).

When my friend Buddy Owens of Maranatha Music first started producing records, he had one goal in mind: He wanted to make Christian music sound better. If he could successfully accomplish his goal, Buddy believed he would fulfill his destiny in God's eyes.

Then Buddy set his sights a little higher. He wanted to be the best producer in Christian music. My friend did as most of us do. We think of our destiny in God's kingdom as climbing a ladder of success, linking our satisfaction to our accomplishments. At each level we expect to achieve greater happiness and fulfillment. But God thinks differently.

One day, after Buddy had experienced a series of setbacks, God finally got his attention. Buddy received fresh insight into his eternal purpose while fellowshiping with the Holy Spirit. He realized his purpose in life was not to become the best Christian music producer, but to produce music that encourages and enables people to worship God. Buddy said, "I don't think I would have ever produced a worship album if God hadn't shaken my career's building blocks. I probably would have only pursued goal-oriented artists, musicians who had their eye on making it to the top, because that's where I wanted to be."

Since then my friend equates his success to directing people to God through the music he produces. It's how Buddy fulfills his ministry of reconciliation. He sees his destiny in the Body of Christ with an eye on eternity. So must we.

A Promise to Obey and Love

Since the beginning, God has destined us to be in a covenant relationship with Him and enjoy the blessings that result from such a relationship. In a covenant relationship, each party gives to the other all they have. Covenants are made so that the needs of one party are met by the strengths of the other, and vice versa. A covenant relationship could be described by the phrase, "What's mine is yours, and what's yours is mine." It's a relationship in which everyone's needs are met.

Our covenant friendship with God is a little different than a covenant relationship with any other person. First, our earthly friends can realistically meet only *some* of our needs. God is the only friend who completely understands us and can meet *all* our needs (Philippians 4:19).

Second, in our earthly friendships we lovingly meet the needs of others to the best of our ability. But God, our ultimate Friend, has no needs. He is totally self-sufficient apart from anything we can do for Him or bring to Him. Our role in our covenant friendship with God is simply to love and obey Him. This is how we bring beauty to the Master Florist's bouquet.

Consequently, there is only one thing that can prevent us from experiencing our covenantal blessings: disobedience to the Master Florist. When we fail to obey God we cut ourselves off from God's promised blessings and suffer as a result, just as flowers in a vase wither quickly when their stems fail to reach the water.

History is strewn with the wilted lives of those who chose to be disobedient. Adam and Eve disobeyed God and forfeited their intimate friendship with Him and the blessings of living in the garden. Their punishment was to labor instead of rest, to sorrow instead of rejoice, and to strive instead of live in contentment.

The Israelites were destined to enjoy the prosperity, peace, and rest in the Promised Land because they had covenanted with God. God told them that if they kept His commands He would bless them more than any other people—physically, socially, financially, and spiritually (Deuteronomy 7:9-15). In return they were to obey Him by following His law, which Jesus summarized in these words: "'Love the Lord your God with all your heart and with all your soul and with all your strength and with all your mind'; and, 'Love your neighbor as yourself'" (Luke 10:27). It was a covenant of love. God would pour out His love to Israel as they poured out their love to Him and others. The Law outlined God's commands for maintaining a right relationship with Himself and with other people.

But the children of Israel chose to disobey God's love commandments. They diluted their love for God with idolatry, and they spoiled their love for each other with hatred and jealousy. So they did not fully experience the blessings of the Promised Land. They wandered in the wilderness for 40 years. Once settled in Canaan, every time the Israelites failed God through disobedience they paid the price, often at the hands of an enemy nation. Finally Israel's continuing disobedience led to their captivity.

Since the cross of Jesus, God's people are referred to as the body of Christ or the church. We are also promised blessings if we obey God by loving Him and others. But the blessings God promises in our covenant relationship with Him are not confined to a geographical area. Our inheritance is the kingdom of

God. Paul describes God's kingdom as a place of "righteousness, peace and joy in the Holy Spirit, because anyone who serves Christ in this way is pleasing to God and approved by men" (Romans 14:17). Once again, our part in the covenant is defined in terms of right relationships: loving friendship with God and with other people.

Our role in this loving covenant, however, is slightly modified from that of the Old Testament saints. Because our friendship with God includes fellowship with the Holy Spirit, we are now able to love in a greater capacity than those who lived before the Spirit was poured out. We no longer are limited to human love. We can choose to express God's unconditional love toward the friends in our lives.

Love is not an option in God's kingdom. Jesus said, "A new command I give you: Love one another. As I have loved you, so you must love one another" (John 13:34). Being a friend to everyone—family members, friends, enemies, and strangers, Christian and non-Christian alike—is an act of obedience to God. It is our part of the covenant of love. If we want to continue to enjoy the blessings of righteousness, peace and joy in God's kingdom, we must love and obey God by being a loving friend to others.

The kingdom of God operates under the law of love. Paul wrote, "Love is the fulfilling of the law" (Romans 13:10). And the law of love must govern our heart, mind, and body—our entire life. Love is defined by 12 attributes in 1 Corinthians 13:4-7 which make up a checklist for a healthy garden of friends.

- Love shows kindness to others, always with patience.

- Love is not envious or jealous of others.

- Love is not proud or boastful.

- Love is not rude to others.

- Love is not manipulative or self-seeking.

- Love does not get angry at others.

- Love keeps no record of wrongs others have done to us.

- Love does not rejoice when evil things happen to others but rejoices when truth prevails.

- Love always offers protective support to others experiencing difficulty.

- Love always trusts or believes in God's Word.

- Love always hopes in the promises in God's Word.

- Love always perseveres in difficult times.

All these attributes must be part of our relationships with God and with each other. We will examine each attribute in greater detail in Part Two of this book.

The value we place on our friendship with God is revealed by how we maintain our garden of earthly friends. Jesus said, "If you love me, you will obey what I command" (John 14:15). If we obey His command to extend unconditional love to others, it proves that we deeply value our friendship with God. If we are inconsistent in our love for others, it reveals that our friendship with God is not our highest priority.

Then Jesus addressed the result of loving others: "If you obey my commands, you will remain in my love, just as I have obeyed my Father's commands and remain in his love. . . . You are my friends if you do what I command. I no longer call you servants, because a servant does not know his master's business. Instead, I have called you friends, for everything that I learned from my Father I have made known to you" (John 15:10, 14,15). As we obey God's command to love others unconditionally, it proves that we are in a love relationship with God and that Jesus Himself looks upon us as His friends.

We often question or rationalize the words of Paul when he wrote to the Romans, "We know that in all things God works for the good of those who love him, who have been called according to his purpose" (Romans 8:28). This is a covenantal promise. When we choose to be a friend to God and to the people He brings into our lives, we will experience the blessings of God (1 John 3:21-24). As friends of God we can expect the Master Florist to be our Healer, Deliverer, Provider, Shepherd, Counselor—and the list goes on. In essence, we expect Jesus to come through for us as a good Friend during life's battles.

But we must realize that these are all *covenantal* attributes, and all will result in God's blessing. However, we need to be fulfilling our part of the covenantal relationship: We must obey the law of love. The blessing of "all things God works for the good" is for "those who love him" (Romans 8:28). How much we love God is reflected by the degree we express His love to our friends for the purpose of pointing them to Him.

Blessings come with obedience. And one of the greatest blessings of our commitment to obey God and love others is that our gardens will be blessed with flourishing friendships.

**Loving a World of Friends
One at a Time**

Many today are looking and praying for a world-wide revival, a dramatic, sudden reconciling to God of masses of people. We often marvel at the early church's vibrant experience of Christianity. The first-century believers turned the world upside-down for God. With the Holy Spirit just as available today, we wonder why people around us aren't being converted by the hundreds and thousands as they were in the book of Acts.

The world is not experiencing masses of people being reconciled to God because we as individuals are not extending our lives in love to strangers, friends, neighbors, and family members. We are not fulfilling our destiny as ministers of reconciliation by being loving friends to those who need to be reconciled and those who need to grow to maturity. The answer to worldwide revival is in our individual commitment to love unconditionally the people God brings into our garden.

Demonstrating love to those in our garden is something we learn to do by choosing to walk in love one day at a time. Every morning, afternoon, and evening we must choose to love. The more we learn to express God's love to others, the more we become accountable to point them to the Lord and nurture them in His love as they grow.

Blessings come with obedience. And one of the greatest blessings of our commitment to obey God and love others is that our gardens will be blessed with flourishing friendships.

PART TWO

Loving Your Garden of Friends

CHAPTER SIX

Dealing with Differences in Your Garden

My friend Joan had been aware for some time that something was missing in her life. She had accepted Christ as her personal Savior and was being led by the Spirit. She read her Bible and prayed daily and attended church regularly. She was doing everything she felt was necessary to have an ideal relationship with God and the people He brought into her life. What could possibly be wrong?

Finally she sought the advice of a trusted confidant. He gave her a simple exercise to complete. In one column on a sheet of paper she listed the names of all the people she regularly came in contact with: family, friends, coworkers, neighbors, etc. In another column she listed the 12 attributes of love found in 1 Corinthians 13:4-7: "Love is patient, love is kind. It does not envy, it does not boast, it is not proud. It is not rude, it is not self-seeking, it is not easily angered, it keeps no record of wrongs. Love does not delight in evil but rejoices with the truth. It always protects, always trusts, always hopes, always perseveres."

Taking one attribute at a time, Joan went down her list of names. Her assignment was to evaluate her relationship with each person. Anyone to whom she did not display a particular attribute of love was to be crossed off her list. Before she even finished the list of traits, all the names had been scratched off. Joan realized she displayed many different traits of love to each person on her list. But she didn't display every trait to every person.

As Joan reviewed the results of the exercise, a sobering reality began to dawn on her: The emptiness she was sensing reflected the fact that her love for the people around her was incomplete. Just because she didn't hate these people didn't necessarily mean she loved them. She had taken love in her relationships for granted.

Like Joan, we are often unfulfilled in our relationships because we mistakenly think that, just because we're Christians, the traits of love listed in 1 Corinthians 13:4-7 pour out of us automatically. In a sense, we're like the people who attend church Sunday after Sunday believing that spiritual transformation takes place by osmosis without any real commitment to Jesus. We assume that our familiarity with 1 Corinthians 13 means that our relationships will be marked by all of love's wonderful attributes without a specific commitment on our part to exercise them.

This is why so many of us feel like we are scratching out our existence in a wilderness of relationships instead of enjoying the wonderful garden of friends we desire. Without an abundance of love, friends are few and far between. Conflicts seem to be abundant. We have yet to understand that the self-disclosure, affirmation, fellowship, and sharing of dreams and goals which make a healthy friendship must be cultivated through a commitment to unconditional love. And nowhere in Scripture do we get a clearer, more specific breakdown of the elements of unconditional love than in 1 Corinthians 13.

Your commitment to exercise every quality of love listed in this passage will equip you to function as a skilled, confident gardener in the garden of your relationships. By exercising these traits in the power of the Holy Spirit you are clothing yourself fully in the image of Jesus for nurturing friendships. Your commitment to unconditional love will have a direct bearing on whether your life is sparsely or densely populated by precious people you have come to call friends.

The attributes of unconditional love listed in 1 Corinthians 13:4-7 form a divinely inspired checklist to help us evaluate our maturity as gardeners of healthy friendships. In the next several chapters we will explore this passage phrase by phrase to discover ways to improve our skills at lovingly nurturing our gardens of friends.

Variety in Your Garden of Friends

The first attribute on our checklist of love's qualities is, "Love is patient, love is kind" (v. 4). Why do these two qualities head the list? Because we need an abundance of patience and kindness in dealing with the many different kinds of people we identify as our friends.

Just as a garden usually contains many different varieties, sizes, and colors of flowers, our gardens of friends are planted with people having different personalities, needs, strengths, and weaknesses. Sometimes these differences make friendships a challenge. At times our friends can be annoying, demanding, stubborn, or otherwise difficult to be around. Without patience and kindness, we would never get to the rest of the list with our friends. We would uproot them at the first sign of disagreement or conflict and toss them on the compost heap of ex-friends.

Sometimes we prefer the translation "Love suffers long" (NKJV) over "Love is patient." "Suffer" paints a more accurate picture of how we feel when coping with friend, family member, or coworker who isn't fulfilling our expectations. We tend to nail ourselves to a cross and declare personal martyrdom. "Woe is me," we moan, thinking we're exercising godly patience.

But human "longsuffering" isn't usually long enough. At some climactic point we come flying off the cross of the suffering saint and turn into vindictive maniacs, screaming, "That's the last straw! Now you're going to get it! Woe is *you!*" Self-pitying martyrdom that ends in explosive retaliation isn't the patience of unconditional love.

The apostle Paul stressed that, at the end of our patience and longsuffering, we must still be kind. To be kind means to show ourselves to be useful or to act benevolently. Godly patience ends in kindness; godly kindness endures patiently.

My friend Nora is an example of these two qualities. Nora's teenaged daughter, Erin, was staying with us one day when my "longsuffering" with my own kids ran short. I was yelling at them unkindly, totally losing it, when I turned to Erin and asked, "Does your mom ever yell at you and your brother?"

"No," she answered. Her reply didn't offer me the solace I was looking for.

Soon Erin's brother Tom stepped in the doorway. I immediately pounced on him with the same question. He replied with a smile, "No, she gets upset and lets us know why, but she never yells at us."

Now if anyone is going to complain about parents yelling at them, it will be teenagers. Erin and Tom's testimony of their mother's patience and kindness became my judge and jury. There I stood, condemned for not being patient and kind with my children. Nora has taught me much throughout our friendship about being patiently kind and kindly patient.

Kindness doesn't mean being a doormat. Sometimes it requires being firm and exercising discipline in love. Even when Christ cleared out the temple with a whip, He never hurt anybody. He scared their sandals off. He confronted their sin. But He spoke and displayed the truth with the backing of love. We also must speak the truth, but do so lovingly and kindly (Ephesians 4:15). Honesty and kindness—the two must be inseparable in everything we say and do.

This guideline particularly applies when our friends display certain patterns of negative behavior. As a friend, you cannot condone or encourage their wrong actions or words by being silent in the name of kindness. You can't let a pouting peony throw her pity parties and expect you to attend, or allow a depressed delphinium to drag you down. Don't let a critical crocus coax you into joining his negative chorus. And don't allow all your energy to be sapped by a starlet sunflower who constantly demands center stage.

Although we can accept our friends' weaknesses, we should not reinforce them. This stance may or may not require us at some *prayerfully* appropriate time to kindly address their negative behavior pattern. An old Arabian proverb says, "A friend is one to whom one may pour out all the contents of one's heart, chaff and grain together, knowing that the gentlest of hands will take and sift it, keep what is worth keeping and with the breath of kindness blow the rest away." If your words or actions hurt your friends, make sure it is because of the conviction you bring to their lives through loving confrontation, not because of any unkindness in your heart.

Different by Design

As you look out over your flower garden, you notice some varieties with large flowers ablaze with color. Others varieties are small and delicate with subtle hues. Some species of flowers grow tall and willowy, while others are short, bushy, close to the ground. Some plants prefer sandy soil, while others grow better in chalky soil or peaty soil. Some crave sunshine; others need shade. Taking time to understand how flowers differ and what they need to reach their potential is vital to cultivating a beautiful garden.

Differences are also apparent in your garden of friends. Perhaps the most notable differences between friends requiring us to lovingly exercise patience and kindness are differences in personality. Some of your friends are talkative; others are quiet. Some are driven workaholics; others are easygoing. Personality types aren't right or wrong, just different. Understanding how your friends differ from you and from each other in personality types and needs, and then exercising patience and kindness in dealing with their differences, is absolutely necessary to helping each one fully blossom.

About 2000 years ago, the Greek physician Hippocrates categorized people by four temperaments: sanguine, melancholic, choleric, phlegmatic. Even though many other methods of distinguishing personality types have been devised over the centuries, we still use Hippocrates' terms today to describe certain behavioral traits. Your ability to relate to your friends patiently and kindly will improve with an understanding of the strengths and weaknesses of these four basic personality types.

Sanguine. These members in your garden of friends might be labeled "talkative tulips." Sanguines are creative, colorful, cheerful. They seem to have more friends than they know what to do with. They're always the life of the party. But their energy drains away quickly. These undisciplined people start with a blast but often do not finish. Their confidence fades quickly. Childish in behavior, sanguines look for credit, make excuses, can't stand criticism, and hate being left alone. So they often seek out a more parental, disciplined personality type—like the melancholy—for a friend or spouse.

Melancholy. These are the "contemplative chrysanthemums" in your garden of friends. Introspective and deeply thoughtful, these schedule-oriented, perfectionists are moved with compassion out of faithfulness and devotion. They are analytical and artistic, and they make friends cautiously. Melancholies sometimes suffer from a persecution complex. They can be critical and unforgiving. They warm to the strengths of the fun-loving sanguine.

Choleric. Cholerics can be distinguished as "pointed poinsettias" among your friends. Cholerics are born leaders—independent, self-sufficient, full of confidence. They continually seek a challenge. Friends are not considered a necessity to them. So they may come across as know-it-alls—bossy, quick-tempered, and demanding of others. They tend to believe the end justifies the means. And when it comes to relationships, usually a phlegmatic is at the end when all is said and done.

Phlegmatic. Phlegmatics are typically "pushover petunias" who are easily pushed around. Relaxed and inoffensive, they get along with most people. That's why phlegmatics often have many friends. But they can dampen enthusiasm in their relationships by being resistant to change. Fearful and worried, phlegmatics shun responsibility while sarcastically judging others who don't. Getting them involved in anything almost requires a bulldozer. This is probably why they are moved into a relationship by hard-driving cholerics.

Another way to illustrate these personality types is to view them as four different kinds of soil. Like the soil in our gardens, personalities don't develop overnight. They are the product of genes, family background, environment, and time. And like the flowers in your garden, your friends exhibit certain traits—some good, some bad—which reflect the kind of personality they acquired over the years.

Sanguines are like porous sandy soil. They warm up quickly in social situations, but their commitment to others drains away just as quickly. The cautiousness and reserve of melancholies likens them to clay soil, cold and sticky. Their tendency toward criticism and unforgiveness sometimes causes them to dry and crack, limiting growth. Sanguines and melancholies get along well when they learn to blend their strengths, forming partnerships that are not too crusty and not too porous.

The sometimes caustic personality of cholerics reminds us of chalky soil. This soil is full of lime, the breakdown of limestone, the building material of great empires. As born leaders, cholerics are great empire builders but often at the expense of others. Easygoing phlegmatics are like spongy, peaty soil. They need some of the initiative found in cholerics, and cholerics need some of the adaptability of phlegmatics. That's why these two personality types often combine to form a fertile, compatible relationship.[1]

If you want certain varieties of flowers to grow in your garden, you need to prepare and enrich the soil so it best accomodates the needs of these plants. Similarly, friendships are more easily formed and maintained when we know what other people want out of life. Each of the four personality types is marked by certain wants. In her book, *How to Get Along with Difficult People*, Florence Littauer says, "The sanguine wants attention and credit. The melancholy wants order and discipline. The choleric wants action and obedience. The phlegmatic wants peace and quiet."[2]

We can help cultivate friendships with others by identifying their personality types and patiently and kindly seeking to accommodate their differences when it is in our power to do so. For example, make sure your sanguine friends get plenty of attention from you. When your melancholy friends are around, keep things reasonably neat and organized. Allow plenty of activity for the cholerics in your life. And give your phlegmatic friends plenty of space.

This doesn't mean you are constantly changing your personality to fit the friend you're with. You're still you; you have your own unique personality. It just means you must take care to enrich the soil around your friends as much as possible with those conditions that will help them grow.

Difficulties with Differences

It is natural for people with opposite personality types to attract one another at first. Yet as time goes by, the very traits that once fascinated us often drive us absolutely crazy. That's when we must realize that people with annoying personality traits aren't weird or wrong, just different. And that's when we must actively commit ourselves to practicing patience and kindness toward those whose personality types aren't always compatible with ours.

We tend to prefer people who are more like us than different from us. We generally have a healthy comfort zone when it comes to others of our personality type. When we meet someone who is compatible with us, we say, "It seems like I've known you all my life." But if we meet someone who doesn't seem to mesh with us easily, our first reaction is, "She's being difficult." It's amazing that the difficult people always seem to be somebody else. Sometimes the difficult person we are dealing with is ourselves.

When we only see another person's differences, difficulties, or weaknesses, it's usually because we're focusing too much on ourselves. Our major concern is "What can she possibly do for me?" or "What am I going to get out of this relationship?" This self-centeredness may be a natural tendency, but it is not the most rewarding. This approach to relationships will leave your garden of friends rather vacant.

Florence Littauer puts it this way: "We've spent 10 years learning to look out for number one, but all we've come up with is people who no longer make an effort to get along with anyone else. It's always the other person's fault. If you don't like the way I function, then get out. So people have gotten out."[3]

We are not meant to be live in exclusive gardens of relationships where only those most like us are welcome. Rather, it is God's desire that our lives flourish with friends of differing personality types. This will only happen when we exercise godly patience and kindness by accepting people as they are, understanding their weaknesses and focusing on their strengths.

Accepting Weaknesses, Nurturing Strengths

Why should we accept our friends' weaknesses and nurture their strengths? Because we need acceptance and nurturing from them. Ministering acceptance and nurture to others qualifies us for the blessings promised in Luke 6:38: "Give, and it will be given to you. A good measure, pressed down, shaken together and running over, will be poured into your lap. For with the measure you use, it will be measured to you." Disciplining ourselves to be patient and kind with our friends is in our best interest. We can expect to receive the abundant blessings of patience and kindness in our other relationships.

Furthermore, there is great blessing in helping friends turn their weaknesses into strengths. But this requires caring enough to find out what makes these people tick. You need to be close friends so they will trust you to look out for their best interests. If you haven't developed a close, trusting relationship, your words may come across as criticism or manipulation,

serving only to reinforce the weaknesses. If your relationship is not at an intimate level, the best thing to do
is to pray for your friends and avoid confronting them
about their weaknesses until your relationship develops
deeper trust.

My husband Rich and I have been good friends
with Harold and his wife Judi for a long time. Our children are about the same ages. We share a lot of similar
interests, like enjoying God's great outdoors. We have
been through a lot together.

At the beginning of our relationship we learned
that Harold had grown up with little confidence in himself. His father constantly drilled into him, "Harold,
you'll never amount to much because you're lousy at
handling money. If you're ever going to do anything
with your life, you'd better stick to sports." So as a
young man Harold concentrated on making it big in
sports. A skiing accident, however, cost him a spotlight
in the Olympic Games, further reinforcing his sense of
worthlessness.

A bankruptcy early in his business career caused
Harold to doubt that he could ever be financially successful. He was afraid he and Judi would never rise
above a very simple existence. They were resigned to
living in rented apartments, just making ends meet.
Many times there was not enough money, especially
when Harold's boss was late in paying him.

Harold seemed to find his niche as a salesman
for a travel agency. His knack for sales along with a
high level of integrity and diligence gained him a large
core of loyal customers. But despite Harold's success,
his boss closed the business after six stormy months,
owing Harold three weeks of commissions which he

never received. At this low point in his life, the words of Harold's father echoed loudly in his mind: "You're a nobody in business."

Desiring to bless our friends by nurturing their strengths and helping them overcome their weaknesses, Rich and I suggested that Harold and Judi open their own travel business. After all, Harold already had a base of customers who trusted him. The four of us met and talked and prayed, and finally came up with a plan that seemed right. The only thing missing was the money to pay our friends' outstanding bills and get the business rolling.

Rich and I prayed and received peace about proceeding to the next step. We decided to give them the money they needed to meet their financial commitments and start the business. But we didn't want this gesture to change our relationship. Proverbs 22:7 says, "The borrower is servant to the lender." We didn't want Harold and Judi to be our servants. So we specified that the money was not a loan but a gift. It was a way we could bless our friends. If they eventually felt directed to repay us, it would be their opportunity to return the blessing. We hoped our gesture would encourage Harold to believe in his own financial ability.

The next phase required God's supernatural intervention. Harold needed to receive credit from the airlines and other vendors—not just a little credit, lots of credit. We prayed for customers, contacts, and credit for the new business. And God moved miraculously. Suddenly, companies that had turned him down were now calling Harold and offering credit.

In response to Harold and Judi's hard work and creative ideas, the business took off. In one year their income increased 600 percent, and their earnings rose into the six figure range. After a year and a half our friends had paid back the money we had given them. Strengthened by our friendship, Harold began to rise above his father's judging words. It was obvious that his loving, heavenly Father was at work in his life and the business.

Rich and I took great care not to step into God's place as we sought to bless Harold and Judi. Too often friends step into His place by manipulating their relationship with others. Sometimes they want more respect out of the friendship. Or maybe they want the person in need to feel obligated to them. We never wanted Harold and Judi to feel obligated to us. Instead, Rich and I wanted Harold to see himself as God saw him and to know God as his Provider. We wanted Harold to believe God would perform miracles in the area of financial weakness if Harold would offer the Lord his strengths.

We all need God's intervention if we are to be the kind people He wants. One of the best ways He intervenes is through His children, the friends in our garden. That's why God tells us to "spur one another on toward love and good deeds" (Hebrews 10:24). We need to ask God to use us to nurture our friends' strengths so they will be challenged to nurture others. This is exactly what happened with Harold and Judi. Rich and I helped them, and they began to help others. Harold shared with his church group his testimony of how God turned his weaknesses into strengths through the patient prayers and kind encouragement of his friends. Now he is encouraging others, turning their weaknesses into strengths by pointing them to God.

Learning from the Strengths of Others

Another blessing we can receive as we exercise patience and kindness toward our different friends is learning from their strengths. Many times God will show us how to strengthen our own weaknesses by observing the strengths of our friends. For example, if your friend is a more dominant sanguine personality, she probably has lots of really terrific ideas and enjoys getting other people involved and enthusiastic. Somehow, though, you never hear about the completion of any of them, because another "great idea" has come along and sent her in another direction.

If you are a primarily choleric personality like me, that will drive you nuts! After all, we cholerics can single-handedly see a project through to the end—no matter what!

But instead of concentrating on the fact that your sanguine friend has dropped the ball again, you can learn something from her about building enthusiasm in others to help get a project done as a group. Having several people involved brings fresh ideas a choleric may never even consider. Over the years my very choleric personality has become more balanced through the love of my many friends and family. Life is much more enjoyable for me now and for those around me because I have become more balanced.

Balance is an important part of identifying the personality types of our friends. One disadvantage in studying personality types is the tendency to permanently label people as one type or another. We insist, "She's a phlegmatic and I'm a sanguine. She'll never fit in my garden of friends. We're just not compatible." We must remember that, although each of us may tend toward one personality type, we also possess quite a smattering of traits from the other three categories. There's a lot more compatibility between the types than we may think.

Also, rigid labeling limits our ability to recognize changes God is affecting to bring greater balance to all our lives. When we exercise godly patience and kindness in the face of our differences and weaknesses, we will learn to nurture and combine our strengths to develop a challenging and beneficial variety in our garden of friends.

Our supreme example for ministering patience and kindness to our friends is Jesus Christ, the bedrock of our gardens, and how He lovingly tended the garden of His relationships. Constantly sought by crowds of people, Jesus chose to concentrate on their needs rather than His own. While the center of attention, He focused on the hurts of individuals, whether a blind beggar, a woman with an issue of blood, or a rich tax collector. Instead of exalting Himself, the Rose of Sharon preferred to wash the feet of His close friends with the water of humility.

Rather than criticize Peter for his shortcomings after His arrest, Jesus reassured His close disciple with the knowledge that He had prayed for Peter and that great things were ahead for him. Jesus understood completely the weaknesses of others. He allowed Himself to be crucified and then rose from the dead to serve our greatest need: forgiveness for sin. Jesus is truly the Lily of the Valley.

Our lives constantly need to be enriched with the patience and kindness of Jesus. As we learn to view our friends and their differences through His eyes, we are better able to maximize their strengths and minimize their weaknesses. Your patience and kindness will cause the wide variety of friends in your garden to flourish.

CHAPTER SEVEN

Why Do We Sometimes Treat Our Friends like Weeds?

Ever since the Garden of Eden, havoc has been created in healthy gardens of friends when people fail to apply the next attribute of love from 1 Corinthians 13:4-7: Love does not envy. Envy here means to be moved with jealousy. Satan envied God's authority and wanted to undermine His friendship with Adam and Eve. His jealousy moved him to approach the couple disguised as a caring friend and tempt them to doubt and disobey God. When they did, man's fellowship with God and ideal harmony with one another was destroyed. Today, jealousy between friends continues to ruin friendships when allowed to grow unchecked.

Jealousy often occurs when we feel we are losing friends. We feel threatened when people we cherish seem to be outgrowing our friendship and moving on to greener pastures. We envy the attention they lavish on others instead of us. Unable to accept our friends' flowering in other gardens, we begin to see them as weeds.

Jealousy often occurs when a person resists or fails to recognize the success God is allowing in the life of another. When friends seem just ready to blossom with all their talents and strengths, what often happens? We do not recognize our friends for who they are becoming. Instead of feeling wonderful for them, we sometimes feel jealous. We envy the progress in their lives instead of rejoicing in it.

Envy Uproots Friendships like Weeds

When we allow envy and jealousy to color our perception of a relationship, we will begin to exclude those persons from our garden of friends by pulling them up by the roots and tossing them away. I watched this happen between Brian and Ken, two good friends who sang together in a Christian group. Brian was the most talented member of the group, and he sensed the Lord directing him to leave the group to minister as a soloist. When Brian told the others they all encouraged him—all except Ken. Ken criticized Brian's plan, accusing him of being selfish. In reality, Ken was jealous that God had gifted and elevated Brian instead of him.

Being sensitive to his friend's feelings, Brian delayed his departure from the group for over a year. But Ken only became more irritated and critical. Finally Brian departed the group with the other members' blessing. But nothing he said or did could eliminate the jealousy in his long-time friend and companion. A new singer was hired to replace Brian, but Ken's bitterness prevented him from working with the new man. Soon the group dissolved. Ken's jealousy was never resolved, and he is no longer singing, having changed careers entirely.

This story illustrates the stages we go through in uprooting friends when envy and jealousy overpowers unconditional love. One of the first warning signs of jealousy is irritability. If you find yourself irritated with friends for no apparent reason, you need to look for areas where jealousy may be crowding out your love for them.

Irritability often leads to criticism, which is meant to diminish the appearance or position of another. Instead of encouraging and nurturing our friends, we criticize their words, actions, or other relationships in a subtle attempt to discredit them and justify ourselves. When we criticize our friends we are playing right into the hands of Satan, the chief critic in this world, the accuser of the brethren (Revelation 12:10). Ever since his fall, Satan has been trying to get our heavenly Father to see His children as nothing more than an overgrown patch of weeds. If we are not careful, we will see each other the same way.

In his book, *Make Anger Your Ally*, Dr. Neil Clark Warren suggests that, when we criticize or attack others, we are evaluating their lives by our own standards. And when they fall short, we treat them with less respect, and that damages the friendship. What's worse, if our friends agree with the process and the verdict of our criticism, they are doubly humiliated and hurt. By the time we're finished, our friends have a difficult time recognizing or appreciating any of their own physical or spiritual progress.[1]

Criticism unchecked grows into judgment. We judge when we attempt to transfer the cause of our jealousy to another. For example, instead of owning up to and dealing with his negative feelings, Ken blamed his problem with the singing group on Brian for leaving. Blaming and judging others for our own problems can pull even the most enduring friendships up by the roots.

Finally, people who allow jealous irritation, criticism, and judgment to overpower their love for a friend end up bitter. And, as with Ken and the singing group, bitterness eventually leads to a parting of the ways between friends.

The Nurture of Loving Encouragement

How do we prevent envy, jealousy, criticism, and judgment from uprooting our friendships? By becoming encouragers. Love doesn't envy; love encourages. Encouragement is part of being a good friend. It means looking for strengths, talents, and godly attributes in our friends and encouraging our friends to improve and refine their positive traits.

Being an encourager means looking for opportunities to recognize progress in a friend. We need to discipline ourselves to look closely at our friends and discover how much they have grown into the character of Jesus. Often our friends don't realize a positive change that has taken place in their character unless we point it out to them.

Frequently I find myself encouraging one of my long-time friends in the middle of a conversation. We're talking and suddenly I realize how much she has advanced in a particular area or how much her life has changed. When I notice something, I make sure to stop and tell her the progress I see. I take her back to an old circumstance in her life and compare it to where she is now.

Noticing and encouraging character traits and growth is not the same as complimenting someone on the nice clothes she wears or the way she does her hair. We tend to major in compliments and forget about encouragement. We need to be as conscientious about how our friends are growing inside as how they look outside.

Sometimes we think that we are encouraging our friends when we offer constructive criticism. We assume that by putting the word constructive in front of the word criticism we somehow make it a positive experience. Not so. These two words form an oxymoron. They contradict each other. Constructive means leading to improvement; criticism implies disapproving judgment. The former nurtures; the latter uproots. Constructive criticism doesn't encourage; it often discourages.

The words we speak can create life or cause death in a relationship (Proverbs 18:21). That's why we must be careful of what we say to people and how we say it. Our words must be saturated with love, designed to encourage and edify, not condemn or accuse. That's what Jesus did. The temptation to "encourage" someone through constructive criticism is a good indication of harbored jealousy.

Recently, God convicted me of this. Martha is a close friend who is very successful in business. She is someone to whom God told me to commit my friendship.

Over the years I witnessed that Martha's life did not revolve around her husband and children. At the ring of the phone she would be off traveling or conducting business. Her children were often left in the care of her husband or other family members.

Though she and her husband had agreed to this arrangement, it irritated me greatly. It is so contrary to my lifestyle. In fact, for most of my life I have been responsible either for my siblings or for my own children. Centering my life on family translated into putting my own needs and desires on the shelf. It is something I came to accept as normal. And so I judged Martha's behavior as abnormal.

So I decided to pray about it. Surely the Lord would have me show Martha the selfishness of her ways. Instead He revealed to me the jealousy in my own heart. I was jealous of Martha because I was unable to enjoy the freedom she enjoyed. I harbored resentment toward her because she was experiencing something I had not. And this irritation led me to criticize her behavior in my heart and to my husband. Of course, I disguised this criticism as "concern" for her children.

But my attitude had driven a wedge between Martha and me. It kept me from being totally comfortable around her. I couldn't hide it; she sensed it too. But God didn't allow the wedge to stay. He knew my heart. More than anything in the world I wanted a close relationship with Him. During a sleepless night of soul-searching He revealed to me the real problem. I became painfully aware that I am capable of falling into sinful backbiting unless I continually check my motives and focus on being an encourager.

Lying there in bed I was ashamed of my actions and feelings. My jealousy had limited my ability to encourage Martha and cultivate our friendship to its fullest potential. There was only one course of action that was acceptable. The Lord showed me that I had to ask Martha's forgiveness for the jealousy that had poisoned my heart. I did, and we have freely encouraged each other to grow since then.

When You Feel Uprooted by Jealous Criticism

It's one thing to take a stand against jealousy in your heart and discipline yourself to be an encourager in your relationships. It's another thing to be the victim of jealousy and criticism in a friendship and know how to respond in a way that nurtures instead of uproots.

I speak from experience. My friend Susan and I were very close. I uncovered some of my fears and areas of my heart to her that I don't share with many others. I had exposed to her my reticence to get too emotionally attached to anything, preferring to control situations and people in my life. I had shared with her my struggle with being a typical take-charge choleric. Instead of waiting for others to make decisions, I did it for them. I had prayed constantly for God to help me change in these areas. And over the years I had sought Susan's prayers that I would be transformed into the Lord's image.

One day Susan called and informed me that she felt God wanted her to talk to me about some things that had been on her mind for a long time. She believed she had been given insight into aspects of my personality that were harmful to others.

The personality weaknesses she shared with me on the phone that day weren't new to me. They were the very ones I had revealed to her and asked her to pray about. God had been faithfully helping me in these areas, though the changes were coming slowly. Old patterns of behavior don't die easily.

Susan's word devastated me. I asked her if my personality problems were really as extreme as she had portrayed them. She assured me that they were. Her words left me gasping to know who I was. I felt like a fragile blossom that had just been sprayed with poisonous weed killer. I began to question if I had made any progress toward my goal of developing the character of Jesus in my life.

Then Susan dropped the biggest bomb of all. She said she had discussed the matter with many of our mutual friends, and they agreed that Susan's observations were correct. Some had even interpreted my behavior toward others as manipulative. Susan had encouraged these women to speak to me personally, but they preferred to pray for me instead of confront me.

I felt so alone, so betrayed, so uprooted. My friends had talked amongst themselves about my faults instead of coming to me directly. I wanted so much to go to them and rectify any hurt I had caused. But Susan wouldn't release their names.

As a result, I totally withdrew from a whole section of my garden of friends: the friends Susan and I shared together. I no longer knew who I could trust, who truly cared about me. For one whole day my imagination ran wild trying to identify my accusers and straining to remember what I said or did that offended them. It was exhausting. I was just torturing myself.

Susan had no idea how her words affected me. She thought that just by confronting me the situation had been dealt with and everything was fine. But it wasn't. She thought our friendship could continue just like before. But my feelings for her were gone. Established trust vanished. All of a sudden years of friendship crumbled around my feet like dead leaves. I hated it.

God lovingly directed me to Margaret for counsel. She was a spiritually mature woman who also knew Susan. Margaret's commitment to the Lord assured me that I could trust her with the confidential nature of the situation. I also trusted her advice.

My whole purpose in seeking counsel was to get a different perspective. I went with an open heart. I needed to know how much of my problem was me and how much was Susan. Was I simply the victim of my friend's malice, or was Susan's insight the sandpaper God was using to smooth some rough areas in my life? My desire was for God to use the incident as a vehicle to change me, to form me more into His image.

After talking with Margaret, I realized that my approach to Susan over the years had been all wrong. I needed to find a better way to relate to her, a way that took into greater consideration her background and family life. Margaret helped me see that Susan's confrontation was prompted by jealousy which sprang from a sense of inadequacy and unresolved hurts from her childhood. Something in me and my behavior magnified her deep pain and triggered her critical response.

Susan hadn't intended to hurt me. On the contrary, I knew without a doubt that she loved me. She wanted the best for me. She wanted me to grow in all the areas I had revealed to her and asked her to pray about. Yet she had unwittingly set herself up as God to judge the acceptable rate of my growth. She honestly believed that she was God's messenger in my life. She felt responsible for me.

True, we are responsible to love our friends and confront them when they need it, but not to pass judgment. When God truly calls us to confront someone, our heart must be completely broken for this person. There can be no anger, no bitterness, no jealousy, no criticism, no judging. There must be only love, concern, and compassion, almost an aching for them because we see them hurting themselves. But this was not the case with Susan. Although she wasn't aware of it, her confrontation had been angry and critical.

Even though Susan didn't intend to hurt me, I was hurt. She had no idea that our friendship was in jeopardy. But I knew that if I didn't control my response to her criticism and seek God's healing, I could hurt her and destroy our friendship. I had to be very careful not to hold Susan's offense against her. I had to constantly discipline myself in God's Word to keep resentment from permanently uprooting our friendship.

Perhaps you have also experienced the pain of a relationship being damaged or uprooted by a friend's jealousy and criticism. The following steps may be helpful to you in learning how to respond to the hurt and guard the relationship.

Time to Cool Down

After my initial feeling of being hurt and betrayed by Susan, I was angry. The first step in my healing process was dealing with my anger. Susan had no idea I was angry; I never expressed it toward her. Yet we somehow think that "letting someone have it" when we are angry is the right thing to do. We have been taught to believe that "getting it off your chest" is healthy. But according to Dr. Neil Clark Warren, there are many good reasons not to express our anger toward those who offend us.

For one thing, it is very difficult to tell people you are angry with them without communicating blame. "If they think you are blaming them, even if you're not, they may become defensive—and that defensiveness may only escalate the problem."[2]

Furthermore, we may feel that expressing our anger is all that's needed to solve the problem. "Sometimes it's too easy to tell someone you're angry with them. It leads to a kind of superficial process, and neither of you talks about the real problem. If you don't proceed to that deeper work, you gain nothing. . . . I have found that people who are eager to tell others of their anger are frequently looking for superficial solutions."[3]

And a superficial solution is the last thing we need when a problem with a friend arises.

When the hurt feelings in a relationship turn to anger, the first thing to do is pull away for a little while. During this cooling off time the Lord will begin to show you how the situation can be turned into a blessing. Allowing yourself space will give you a different perspective.

But this "holiday" shouldn't last very long; maybe a week or two at the most. Any longer and you run the risk of taking a permanent vacation from the person who offended you. It becomes too easy to ignore the problem by just not seeing each other again. It is difficult to know if you are harboring resentment when there is distance between you. Self-deception can creep in. You begin to believe you have forgiven your friend when all you have done is repress the anger.

I used this cooling off period with Susan to put some things down in black and white about our relationship. This was very therapeutic. I was prompted in my heart to list on paper Susan's true feelings toward me and all the positive things she had added to my life and done for me. I wrote down words she had spoken to me on other occasions that were uplifting. I remembered the times she was there for me when I was down and needed a friend. I thought about the many times I had turned to her as a faithful prayer warrior. I listed the many attributes in her life that I wanted in mine. By the time I was done writing there were pages of positive things Susan had added to my life over the years that far outweighed the one painful experience of being criticized and betrayed by her.

At this point I had to ask myself and God why Susan would risk damaging our relationship by confronting me as she did. After much prayer the answer became clear. For many years Susan had been a doormat to take-charge people in her life like her family and me. She found herself forced into things she didn't want to do and angry at herself for letting them happen. After this resentment built up over a period of years the lid blew off, and her deadly words of criticism sprayed all over the nearest choleric flower in her garden: me, her close friend. She didn't mean to hurt me; she just didn't know how toxic her explosion was.

Through my writing exercise the Lord took my eyes off what I had invested in Susan and helped me focus on what she had invested in me. This prevented me from feeling like a martyr or a victim or thinking that I had been the only one giving in our relationship. The good Susan had brought into my life over the years greatly overshadowed the bad. I realized that the hurt I felt was not the result of a malicious action on her part. By putting things down on paper I could see how much she truly cared for me.

After regaining my perspective during the cooling off period, the Lord encouraged me to take steps to restore the relationship with Susan. I could not allow the hardness of my anger to crack my heart. I had to speak to her on the phone at least once a week.

During this time I found myself a bit reserved toward Susan. I didn't know how to act. The Lord revealed to me that I was not to let her know anything was wrong or talk directly to her about the circumstances. I wasn't going to be phony, but at the same time I wasn't going to act indignantly or play the role of the martyr. So I decided to be kind and friendly. It was the only way to please my heavenly Father in my relationship with Susan.

Practicing Forgiveness

As I began expressing my love to Susan, I also took another helpful step in the healing process. In order to take an honest look at Susan's confrontation with me, I launched into another written exercise. I took a sheet of paper and divided it down the middle. On one side I listed all the negative things she accused me of saying and doing. For each point I asked myself hard questions like, "Is this true? Did I manipulate the situation? Did I force my opinion on someone? Did I demand my way without caring what others wanted?" In the opposite column I wrote down my responses as factually and unemotionally as possible.

Before me in black and white, the answers were either yes or no. A much clearer picture of Susan's criticism developed. I was able to see how much of this painful scenario was Susan's reaction and how much was my own doing. I determined the offenses for which I still needed to ask her forgiveness. And I identified instances where I needed to forgive her. Forgiveness was a key to my healing.

God reminded me about Job in the Bible. Job's well-meaning friends were trying to comfort him during his trials. Yet their motivation strayed from the track of love, and they ended up criticizing him. In response to their criticism, God required Job to pray for his friends (Job 42:10). Job was healed and his prosperity was restored when—and only when—he prayed for those who offended him.

When we choose to forgive, we choose to be obedient to God. Jesus didn't *suggest* that we forgive one another, He *commanded* it (Matthew 6:14,15; Mark 11:25; Luke 6:37; 17:3,4). It's not a matter of forgiving because we feel like it. It's a matter of forgiving because God said we must and because we choose to obey Him.

That's why writing down our hurts and dealing with them in black and white is so important. If Satan ever accuses you of those offenses again or a situation painfully reminds you of your failure or your mind wants to harbor hurt again, you can always relate back to the written proof that those incidents were dealt with. You took care of them by choosing to follow the path of forgiveness.

Finally I was able to write Susan a carefully-worded note. I couldn't support her for sharing confidences with our friends or for the painful way she confronted me. But I did thank her for being a friend, for being willing to confront me at the risk of our friendship. Though I knew it would take a long period of time for my trust in Susan to be restored, I was grateful for what God showed me through this incident. It magnified how destructive criticism is among friends and how healthy and vital forgiveness and encouragement is to healthy relationships.

Friends who are growing in unconditional love are not jealous of one another. Jealousy in friendships blinds us to the beautiful uniqueness of each individual. We fail to appreciate and respect the gifts, abilities, and talents God has given each of us. Instead, we become defensive of our own gifts and critical of what God has given others. And self-centered behavior like that is death to a friendship.

But as we learn to lovingly forgive each other's failures and weaknesses and encourage each other's strengths, jealousy and criticism will no longer distort our perception of each other. And when your garden of friends is free of these pollutants, you and your friends have room to grow and flourish.

CHAPTER EIGHT

Tear Down the Walls That Shut Friends Out

Finally the time has come. You spent all morning in preparation. Makeup and nails are flawless. Every hair is in place. Clothes are perfect. A ring of the doorbell and soon the whole world will know you have arrived. The door opens slowly. The doorkeeper greets you with a smile. Not a word is spoken as he ushers you through the house and into the garden, an endless sea of green grass dotted with the brightest flowers you have ever seen.

It is the ultimate garden party. And you were invited. How exciting! Your eyes want to drink in all the beauty. Slowly you start inspecting the individuals who make up the beautiful sea of color. After all, doesn't the host want you to select a few of these people for your own garden of friends?

In the secrecy of your mind you pull out your own list of qualifications and begin making comparisons. *Let me see, that one will never do. Her lipstick doesn't match her dress. Must not be well-bred socially. Certainly doesn't spend a lot of money on her clothes. And listen to him. High school education at the most. Probably holds some mindless job somewhere. And that one over there. A total snob. Acts as if she owns the place. Well, she's not going to get any satisfaction out of rejecting me.* You look away disinterestedly to avoid eye contact.

Suddenly your host is standing before you. Clearing your throat, you say, "Lord, how nice of you to invite me. What a beautiful garden you have."

His compassionate, loving eyes fix on yours as if to read your soul. He says, "Every flower in my garden, including you, is a masterpiece, a work of art. All are equally beautiful in my eyes. Yet you seem to find few that meet your lofty standards. And your garden of friends is sparsely populated as a result. If you will discard your list of qualifications and regard each individual as I do, you will soon find your garden overflowing with wonderful friends."

This scene is fictional, of course. But perhaps it has a ring of truth from your experience. Why is it that we suddenly shut down toward certain people before even saying hello? Why do some people never have a chance of being our friend? What's behind these "No Trespassing" signs on our garden gates?

The next guideline for healthy friendships on our checklist from 1 Corinthians 13:4-7 gives some insight: Love doesn't boast; love isn't proud. Boasting in this verse means sounding your own praises, tooting your own horn. Pride here means having an inflated idea of your own importance. Both of these terms picture the person who feels and acts superior to others. Superiority can be reflected in how we think and communicate about our family heritage, wealth, personal appearance, intellect, education, holiness, success, independence, power, or social status.

The apostle Paul warned us in Romans that an attitude of superiority is wrong: "Do not think of yourself more highly than you ought, but rather think of yourself with sober judgment, in accordance with the measure of faith God has given you" (12:3). It is the opposite of unconditional love which welcomes and serves all. The superiority of pride is like a closely guarded, narrow gate, keeping out all those who don't measure up to our standards or fit our comfort zone.

How can pride make such a big difference in our relationships? Remember: Pride kept Lucifer, alias Satan, from enjoying his heavenly dominion. He was thrown out of heaven for his attitude of superiority (Isaiah 14:12-14). And at times pride robbed the children of Israel of God's covenant blessings in the Promised Land (Deuteronomy 8:10-14,19,20). Pride will also keep us from receiving God's blessings in our relationships.

Pride doesn't attract friends; it drives them away. But the servanthood of unconditional love opens a wide pathway for others into our lives. By examining ourselves and eliminating pride, we will be open to a wider variety of different flowers in our gardens.

Sometimes pride in its most subtle form appears to be love. We're tempted to express spiritual superiority in holy-sounding ways. Have you ever heard someone say, "God gave me the opportunity to bless so-and-so by giving him such-and-such"? How about, "I've really been praying for you"? Or perhaps, "No wonder the Lord woke me up in the middle of the night to pray for you. Good thing I did."

It is one thing to mention to people that you will pray for them as an act of support. It is quite another to broadcast your spiritual activities or victories because of the underlying desire for recognition of your spiritual maturity or standing with God. You may think such boasting will attract people to your garden, but it doesn't. By elevating yourself through pride you make them feel inferior, even unwanted.

Spiritually proud people are like the Pharisees in Jesus' day. The Pharisees were a religious group who always made a public announcement when they gave to the poor or spent time in prayer (Matthew 6:1-6). In reality, they considered themselves better than others, even better than Jesus. Whenever we consider ourselves too good or too spiritual to associate with someone, and subtly make sure everyone knows it, we exhibit the pride of the Pharisees. Everybody hated the Pharisees, and clinging to pharisaical pride will keep people at a distance from you as well.

Love means voluntarily bending to be a servant, hoping to lift others up. Pride is just the opposite. It causes us to purposely put others down in an effort to appear superior. So how do we get rid of pride? The only way to make sure pride doesn't exclude others from your garden is to continually choose the path of humility and servanthood in your relationships.

Pride and Prejudice

In high school I was fascinated by the captivating presence of my classmate Sally. Sally could attract anybody she wanted. Other classmates knew she would just use them to her advantage. It didn't seem to matter to them. They were mesmerized by her. Boys dropped like flies in her path, and then she stepped on them.

Popular, a cheerleader, and cute, Sally walked down the halls of school with great confidence. Sally knew who she was and what she was capable of doing.

I didn't like Sally. I labeled her a snob, not capable of being a caring friend like me. She was superior to me in many ways, but in my mind I elevated myself above her. I was proud that I was not like her.

My pride followed me into my adult years. Anytime I saw a woman who was extremely confident, attractive, or popular, I immediately labeled her a snob. In my eyes, she used others to her own advantage just as Sally had. I never considered that her confidence may have been based on a relationship with Jesus. Instead, I judged her unworthy of my friendship without a word being spoken between us.

Years later the root of my judgmental pride was exposed. I realized I had been jealous of Sally's popularity and considered anyone who reminded me of her a snob, unworthy of my friendship. Though I sincerely forgave Sally for being Sally and myself for my pride, for years I found that the presence of a confident woman would sometimes trigger my old response. Or I would walk into a room and immediately ask myself, "Who's the most attractive? Who's basking in the most attention?" This reaction often caught me off guard. It has taken a long time to retrain myself to renounce my pride and accept these women at face value with unconditional love.

There is a word for proud superiority that excludes potential friends before we even meet them or get to know them: prejudice. If pride is the gate that only admits a select few to our garden of friends, prejudice is the walls that keep out all who don't qualify on

the basis of our own opinions. In order to live in unconditional love with others and develop healthy friendships, all pride and prejudice must be torn down. This
includes those barriers to relationships we disguise as
our personal preferences in friends.

There is a prominent Christian speaker living in
a very affluent community who maintains such preferences. I'll call her Prescilla. Prescilla's friends don't
choose her; she chooses her friends. And her friends are
a specific type of person. Only the socially elite qualify.

As a child, Prescilla experienced mostly poverty
and few luxuries. Her parents, a husband and wife ministering team, poured out their material resources to
needy people so that scrutinizing Christians could find
no fault with their ministry. When Prescilla grew up she
decided her life was going to be different. She was no
longer going to associate with people from the lower
socio-economic classes. So she has surrounded herself
with wealth and wealthy people, and those who don't
fit her standards are left outside her wall.

Many women are jealous of the friends Prescilla
has chosen. To them the sign on Prescilla's gate reads
"Keep Out." These precious sisters in the Lord feel excluded and rejected, not good enough. They feel inadequate for one reason or another. Though Prescilla may
be friendly to these "outsiders," she refuses to extend
her friendship to them. Instead, she chooses to nurture
a sparse garden of hand-picked friends.

Some would call a narrow focus like Prescilla's
"personal preference," a matter of setting high standards for our lives. Regardless of how we sugar-coat it,
it's still a form of prejudice that functions as a privacy
fence excluding others from our garden. We *should* have
personal standards of excellence for being a good friend

and for maintaining our friendships. But we *should never* establish standards of excellence that others must meet before we let them into our lives as friends. When we do so we set ourselves up as a judge at the cost of rejecting others.

Whether our prejudicial walls are roughly hewn and obvious or smoothly sanded and barely visible, they still inflict pain on others. Prejudice causes open wounds in our relationships. This is contrary to the healing nature of Jesus. He called us to build up or edify those around us with unconditional love, not to injure them with our prejudiced attitudes and actions.

Tearing Down Walls, Building Up Friends

When Dan Robert was making out the list of guests for his wife Patti's birthday party, she insisted on Karen and her husband Ray being included. Dan Robert questioned the wisdom of his wife's decision, reasoning that the party was for close friends only. Besides, he didn't know Karen and Ray very well. Actually, nobody knew Karen and Ray very well.

Karen is in Patti's discipleship group. She is a true servant, always ready to pray for others. Or if someone is home ill, she will cook all day and take a hot meal to the family. Karen is like a sweet-smelling gardenia whose fragrance lingers for a long time—but not long enough for people to remember to include her on their party list! She and Ray never get invited anywhere.

Why? Well, Karen and Ray don't have a lot of money. Their education is limited. Karen is overweight. And their clothes are not stylish. These are the superficial things that seem to matter to people these days when deciding who to invite to a party or include as friends. But they don't matter to Patti. She felt the Lord specifically wanted Karen and Ray to be present. So they were invited.

And what a blessing it was for Karen and Ray. For the first time they could remember they were included in a social activity outside their family. Other guests at the party were surprised at their presence. Some were blessed to see them there, commending Patti for her openness. Karen and Ray would not have been invited to any of Prescilla's parties. But Patti was not about to let barriers of pride and prejudice keep her from welcoming them into her garden. What a testimony of unconditional love!

When we think of social prejudice we usually think of *racial* prejudice. And since many Christians have torn down the walls between them and people of other races, they will insist, "I'm not prejudiced. I'm a Christian." But there are other groups of people to whom many Christians respond by erecting walls of prejudice and posting "Keep Out" signs on gates of pride.

Homosexuals are one such group. When Rich and I had fellowship meetings in our home, there were at least four former homosexual men who attended over the years. One had experimented with homosexuality as a young boy. Another was the victim of sexual abuse by a family member as a child.

The other two men, Randy and Cal, became involved in homosexuality as adults. Their respective homosexual suitors duped them into believing their unsuccessful relationships with women proved they were meant to be homosexuals. Randy and Cal tried the homosexual lifestyle, but it didn't take long for them to realize that homosexuality has no place in God's order.

Even after stopping their homosexual behavior, Randy and Cal felt they were marked for life. They were afraid to talk to others about their mistake. They were convinced that the men in the church would avoid them if their past sins were made known. And their fears were understandable. Unfortunately, many Christians have wrongly labeled homosexuality an unforgivable sin. We act as if the blood of Jesus can cover most sins, but it can't quite cover this one.

Both Randy and Cal labored under a load of guilt because they were Christians when entering into this lifestyle. They condemned themselves for not being stronger or wiser to resist temptation. Satan, the accuser of the brethren, used their past against them to keep them imprisoned in guilt. They needed to know that Jesus' death on the cross for their sins was enough, and that they could get on with their lives, confident they were accepted by God and by His people.

But Randy and Cal felt excluded. They were desperate for understanding and acceptance. They were dying inside until they began experiencing unconditional love from our home fellowship group. In the security of that setting, each of them shared his story with me privately. Had I been prejudiced against homosexuals I would not have been in a position to truly be a friend. Instead, from the love and compassion in my heart I was able to say, "I really don't understand from experience all you're going through. But I do understand you have a need. Please let me help you."

Soon my husband Rich was also accepted into Randy and Cal's confidence. As a Christian man, Rich's response was vital to their healing. They turned to him for prayer and acceptance, which he readily provided. Rich continued to express his acceptance of Randy and

Cal by greeting them with warm hugs. He would not allow a wall of prejudice to spring up to protect him from what God had forgiven and forgotten.

What You Don't Know Can Hurt You

Sometimes walls of prejudice are hinged to our gates of pride by a lack of knowledge. Lack of knowledge corrodes our heart with fear and keeps people from entering freely into our gardens of life.

At an early age I gained an understanding of how lack of knowledge can lead to prejudice in relationships. When I was 12, my mother developed an uncontrollable chemical imbalance in her body. This led to a condition known as manic depression. In the illness's most severe stages, mother had to be hospitalized in a mental institution. But since my father took time to educate my two brothers and me about our mother's condition, it caused no fear in us.

But my mother's mental illness did create fear in some of my friends and their parents. They wouldn't allow their children to play at my house, even though I was allowed in their homes. One mother in particular would ask me potentially explosive questions: Is your mother's illness hereditary? Does she ever get violent? Are you ever afraid of her? If I hadn't been so well-informed by my father, her questions could have easily developed fear in me. Her questions reflected what many others were thinking.

God gave me the ability not to hold their prejudice against them. I realized it was based on lack of understanding and fear of the unknown. There are so many misconceptions regarding mental illness. That's why today my mother talks on radio shows about her illness, answering questions from listeners. It is her effort to tear down prejudice toward those who are mentally ill.

My childhood experience helped me learn early that prejudices come in all shapes and sizes. Some come and go in our lives, like a temporary picket fence. Some resemble a split rail fence with gaps through which acceptable people can crawl. Other prejudices surround us like a fortress designed to keep out all "undesirables." Still others are constructed for the sake of our own privacy, carefully hiding our insecurities and weaknesses.

Then there are those prejudices painted to look so spiritual that they kind of blend into our concept of being Christlike. One day God pointed out one of these "spiritual" prejudices to me. I discovered I was prejudiced against people who were prejudiced. It was hard for me to accept people into my garden if they displayed prejudice toward others.

The Lord convicted me that, as righteous and noble as my view seemed to me, the prejudice of others is no excuse for me to build a barrier. These people need love and understanding too. Many times they don't know they are prejudiced. They were brought up this way, and they lack knowledge. I had to learn to accept these people and humbly, lovingly help them see the walls they erected around their gardens.

Opening Your Garden to All

So how do we discover and destroy the barriers of pride and prejudice that exclude people from our garden? Joan Cavanaugh shared a formula with me that has been helpful. I hope it is helpful to you.

The first step is to *define the problem*. When you are aware of a conflict in a business situation, church

group, family, marriage, or any other relationship, you
need to examine it closely and pinpoint the problem.

In order to define the problem, you need to answer
some hard questions. For example, you're a woman,
and you always seem to have a problem on the job with
your male supervisors. How do you really feel about
men in authority? Or let's say you feel constantly an-
noyed by people of different races or ethnic backgrounds.
What do you actually think about people who are raci-
ally or ethnically different from you? Perhaps you stead-
fastly avoid doing business with Christians. How do
you really feel about Christians in business?

Your answers to these questions will disclose your
prejudices. If your honest answer is, "I hate them," "I
don't trust them," or "I can't stand being around them,"
then you have probably defined an area of prejudice.

Having defined the problem, the next step is to
discover the prejudice. A prejudice is a pre-judged opinion, deciding how you will think or act *before* you have
a clear picture of reality. For example, your problem
may be with a friend who has been out of work three
months. You're angry with him because you feel he's
lazy. Your prejudice may follow this logic: All jobless
people are lazy; Bill doesn't have a job; therefore Bill is
lazy.

Does your prejudice reflect reality? No. Some
jobless people may be lazy, but not *all* of them are. And
it doesn't reflect reality in Bill's case. What you don't
know is that he spends several hours a day tracking
down leads, sending out resumes, and scheduling interviews. He just hasn't been hired yet. Your prejudice
may be a wall keeping Bill out of your garden.

Or you may have a problem with a woman at
church who comes to service wearing too much makeup.

Your prejudicial thinking may be: Worldly women wear too much makeup; Sue wears too much makeup; therefore Sue is worldly. And instead of welcoming Sue into your garden as a sister in Christ you build a wall of prejudice excluding her because she happens to like wearing makeup.

Your prejudices will reveal areas in your life where you are trying to establish your superiority over someone. This is the same mind-set that produces white supremacists, black supremacists, gender supremacists—you name it, the list goes on and on. Our prejudiced lenses will cause us to see people the way we want to see them, not the way they really are.

The only way to be delivered from this superior/inferior mentality is to become principled on the basis of God's Word, which helps us see people through God's eyes instead of our lenses of prejudice. The third step in the formula is *do the principle*. What is the principle? It's the one Jesus gave us: "A new command I give you: Love one another. As I have loved you, so you must love one another. By this all men will know that you are my disciples, if you love one another" (John 13:34,35).

Love is the principle that overcomes all prejudice. Love respects everyone, so principle-minded persons respect everyone and do not regard themselves superior to anyone.

Following the principle of love will cause us to fulfill the fourth phase of the formula: *delete the problem* If we center our lives on the principle of love, the barriers to relationships will come down. Our lives will flourish with flowering friends because we walk in love

Walking in love is a daily walk. Every day we must tear away any vestiges of the walls of prejudice and gates of pride excluding others from our garden. As these rotten beams and planks are consumed by the bonfire of unconditional love for others, it will lift a sweet-smelling sacrifice to our Lord.

CHAPTER NINE

No Stomping or Mowing Allowed

Has something like this ever happened in your garden?

You're gazing out the kitchen window drinking in the beauty of the colorful, well-tended flowers gracing your yard. All the time, energy, and money you've invested in your garden is starting to pay off. Suddenly a soccer ball comes bouncing into view. You fear the worst but are powerless to prevent it. The ball bounds into your flower bed, flattening a few of your lovely zinnias. Seconds later, to your horror, two neighbor boys in the heat of competition race pell-mell into the yard after the ball. You gasp. The boys, completely oblivious to the flowers underfoot, are jostling and kicking and stomping after the ball. Petals fly. Stems and leaves are ground into the sod. Even before you can take a step toward the patio door to drive the intruders off, one scuffing kick has sent the ball flying down the street, and the boys disappear after it.

It only took a few seconds, but the damage is done. A number of your beautiful flowers are bent and bruised. With a lot of care they may recover. But several others are broken off, torn, even uprooted. You'll try your best to save them, but who knows if they'll make it. Your heart aches over the senseless damage done. And it could have been so easily prevented if those thoughtless little boys had been more considerate.

Such thoughtlessness can happen among friends too. Sometimes we carelessly stomp through our garden of relationships and leave a path of destruction. The next attribute of love on our checklist from 1 Corinthians 13 speaks to inconsiderate behavior that flattens friendships instead of nurtures them: Love is not rude.

Rudeness is acting indecently in relationships or embarrassing others, causing people to feel like burying their head in the sand or disappearing off the face of the earth. If given just 10 seconds, you can probably think of a blatant example of embarrassment with your friends—and most likely you were the victim in the incident you remember. But what about the times when you were the perpetrator, stomping carelessly over someone's ideas or feelings? "Who me?" you ask defensively. Yes, unfortunately we all need to be reminded of the importance of building others up instead of trampling them into the ground by being rude.

Cutting Others Down with Sarcasm

One of the ways we are guilty of stomping on friends is through sarcasm. The word is derived from a Greek word meaning to tear flesh or to cut. Often our cutting sarcastic remarks to or about someone are cam-ouflaged as humor. But what's so funny about some-thing that crushes or tears a friend? Remember: If a humorous, cutting remark is not funny to everybody, especially the person being discussed, it's not funny at all. Cutting someone down publicly, even under the guise of humor, is rude and indecent. Unconditional love doesn't treat people that way.

Why are we tempted to cut others with sarcasm? There are usually two reasons. First, sometimes we tend to be overly concerned about how we compare with other people. We feel like we must put someone else down so we can look better. Sarcasm is a convenient way of doing so, especially when it's disguised as humor.

Second, sarcastic stompers don't seriously take into consideration the feelings of others. Insensitivity dulls the pangs of guilt as our friends are crushed by our inconsiderate words and deeds.

When growing up I became very proficient in the arena of sarcasm. Moving from school to school, I learned it could be a very effective defense mechanism. When people hurt me I could rip them to shreds with just a few words. I have been laying this "skill" on the altar before the Lord for years.

Thankfully, He has given me grace to progress immensely toward ridding my life of hurtful sarcasm.

But every once in awhile sarcasm creeps into my heart and I realize that I have verbally walked over one of my precious friends. That's when I have to seek forgiveness from God and my offended friend, knowing just how much I need the Lord to direct my steps among my garden of friends. Sometimes my relation-ship with an offended friend may take a long time to heal. It serves to remind me that being a friend requires the skill of building up with words of love, not tearing apart with cutting sarcasm.

The Lawn Mower of Gossip

Rudeness is often expressed through another means of leveling a lovely garden of friends: gossip. Gossip is information abuse that results in friend abuse. The slashing tongue of gossip is like a lawn mower in a flower bed. It doesn't belong there. Flowers were meant to be cherished not chopped. A few minutes of gossip can destroy years of tender care in a relationship.

Just as sarcasm can be veiled in humor, gossip often sneaks into our garden under a number of disguises. Sometimes it is disguised as genuine concern. It will manifest itself in words like, "I need your advice about so-and-so in order to help them. Let me tell you what I've heard." What follows is potentially hurtful or embarrassing information exchanged under the guise of helpfulness.

Sometimes the lawn mower of gossip cuts through the church under the disguise of "sharing prayer requests." Maybe you have participated in this or perhaps been a victim. The scenario goes like this: Someone comes to you urging you to pray for so-and-so, "and let me tell you why." Then out of their mouth comes a stream of detailed information that makes supermarket tabloids look mild.

Or perhaps the informant doesn't share the details, but creates such a cloud of suspicion around a friend's name, experiences, or reputation that you start speculating on your own. You may pass the report on to others by adding, "You know, I've seen so-and-so do such-and-such, so this must be why she needs prayer" or "Maybe something is wrong with their marriage" or "I really wondered if he was as spiritual as he seemed."

There is another subtle, spiritual-sounding model of gossip often used among friends, particularly in churches. I call it the "council of many." How does this seemingly spotless and shiny model operate? When we feel we have been wronged by someone, we make sure we talk to quite a few people about it. Often our listeners will willingly confirm, "Yes, I heard he did the same thing to so-and-so. You have every right to feel the way you do. He definitely has a problem, and we need to pray about it."

Sharing your hurt with an intimate, discreet friend for prayer and support is often helpful. But indiscriminately sharing personal information with a wide circle of people to gain sympathy and support is gossip.

Innocent Words

Gossip isn't always words spoken maliciously. Sometimes it's just small talk that gets out of hand. Someone tells you something in confidence, but fails to specifically ask you to keep it to yourself. So you feel free to talk about it. Well, you are not free. You are responsible for the words that come out of your mouth whether or not they're malicious and whether or not they were branded "for your ears only." Once those words leave you, you lose control of how the information is used later.

Recently I had a funny reminder of how information can be distorted as it passes from person to person. Our family joined with some friends for a week-long houseboat trip on Lake Mead. Prior to pushing off, our youngest daughter broke the flyswatter, which is a necessity in June!

Spotting our friend Jim still on the shore, I shouted, "Jim, Annie broke the flyswatter. Could you ask the girls to pick one up?"

He replied, "Sure," then turned and called up the hill to Stacy and Amy. "We need a flyswatter from the grocery store." The girls nodded and headed off to the store.

In a few minutes Stacy and Amy returned with what they thought Jim asked them to buy: a bottle of Slice and a jug of water. "Flyswatter" evolved into "Slice/water"—and the flies were thrilled! It's hard to believe such a distortion of words could happen between just three parties within sight of each other in only one or two minutes. This incident illustrated to me the importance of guarding what we say about others. Sometimes an innocent, unguarded comment revealing a tiny confidence can snowball into harmful gossip.

The incident on the shore reminded me of the telephone game most of us played as children. Somebody would make up something funny to say and whisper it to the person next to him. That person then whispered what he heard to his neighbor and so on. By the time the message traveled around the circle it rarely sounded like the original. The information became distorted as it was shared from person to person. By the same token, when we thoughtlessly pass on what we hear about others, we may be contributing to the spread of distorted information.

Potentially damaging or embarrassing information about others may start innocently enough, but let's call it what it is: gossip. And people who carelessly spread this information are gossipers, rudely mowing down others. Regardless of how harmless it may first appear, gossip can shred into tiny pieces the hearts and confidences of even the sturdiest friends in our garden.

If we do not apply the guideline of unconditional love to how we speak to and about our friends, we run the risk of becoming a tool in Satan's hand to wear down the saints. The Scriptures place meddling gossipers right up there with murderers (1 Peter 4:15). It's no wonder. Murderers mow people down physically, and gossipers mow people down emotionally, relationally, and spiritually.

The Gossip Stops Here

One area of gossip God convicted me of is being a passive participant in the gossip of others. I used to sit and listen to angry friends tell how others had offended them instead of asking if they had talked to the offenders about the hurt. Even though we may not agree or disagree with others who share such information with us, by listening to them we may be encouraging them to gossip.

Oftentimes gossipers want us to be just as angry as they are toward the persons they are talking about so they can feel justified in their anger. They don't want us to remind them to forgive and release the offender. They would rather stay offended because forgiveness requires greater sacrifice. But if you go along with gossipers, you have accepted a part in their sin, and you have failed them as a friend as well. A sure way to stall the destructive lawn mower of gossip is to not allow a friend to spread it.

The same holds true in a group. Anytime we are in the company of two or more and the "problems" of a friend not present becomes the topic of discussion, we need to remind the others of our responsibility to love one another by not gossiping. If that doesn't change the subject of the conversation, you should leave. We need to stand up and clearly state our commitment not to gossip. Your Christian friends need more role models in these situations, and you might as well be one. To remain silent and ignore the problem makes you a responsible party in the destruction of other people. Because God has a stake in our relationships with our friends, He holds us accountable to stand up for what's right.

Yet in our responsibility to confront gossip, the Lord still requires us to be gentle with the gossiper. It would be better to say something positive to them instead of snapping, "You shouldn't say that." You don't know where the gossiper is coming from. They are probably hurt and need love more than harsh reprimand. It's very important that we are sensitive to say something positive not only about the person being mowed down by gossip but also to the person who is gossiping.

Instead of gossiping, we need to practice speaking positively about each other in general. It will be extremely healthy for your garden of friends. Let's say you see something positive happening in Jane's life. So you tell Helen about it: "Isn't it great what God is doing for Jane. And Helen, if He can do it in Jane's life, then He can do it in your life too." In turn Helen will be inspired to pass the good news about Jane on to someone else. And eventually it will get back to Jane.

As a result, you will build up a healthy array of friends who trust you. It is encouraging to a friend to be complimented and affirmed by you in person. But it can be even more encouraging to hear those compliments from you and others through the grapevine. This kind of positive speaking to and about one another builds commitment and loyalty in friendships.

My precious friend Nancy shared with me something that happened during a prison chapel service where she was ministering that helped her put a stop to gossip among her friends. One of the men stood up during the service and began to talk about gossip. He said that, since there's not much to talk about in prison, gossip easily becomes the number one daily activity. However, he was upset that the inmates who said they loved Jesus continued to gossip.

He related that he began telling his brothers in the Lord who started to gossip to him, "I want you to know that everything you tell me about this brother I am going to tell him." He said his statement turned their engines off, just shut down gossip among the Christian inmates. The lashing tongue of gossip no longer functioned as a destructive lawn mower among those brothers.

When Nancy heard the effectiveness of this prisoner's solution, she determined to do the same thing in her garden of friends. She announced it as her official policy at the ladies' Bible study she was teaching. It produced the desired effect.

Maybe you need to take a similar stand among the friends in your garden and shut down the lawn mower of gossip for good.

CHAPTER TEN

Be a Giver Instead of a Taker

According to classic Greek legend, Narcissus was a very beautiful but rather aloof young fellow. Even though lovely nymphs threw themselves at him, Narcissus was not impressed. He rejected everyone—everyone, that is, except himself. One day he caught a glimpse of his own reflection in a quiet pool. Instantly he became totally infatuated with the wonderful image and fell in love with himself.

Completely enthralled with his own image, Narcissus longed for his newfound love. He spoke to his reflection, but there was no response. His love was unsatisfied. Whenever he tried to lovingly touch the magnificent mirror image of himself, it was shattered by ripples. Eventually Narcissus pined to death. The nymphs desired to burn his body, but it disappeared. From the earth where he was last seen grew the native garden flower of the eastern Mediterranean: the narcissus.

Today the term "narcissism" carries some rather negative connotations. Narcissism is an obsessive love of self that causes a person to be completely self-centered. A person possessing this trait in some degree will find it difficult to follow the next condition on our checklist for a healthy garden of friends: Love is not self-seeking.

Most of us fail to see ourselves as self-seeking or self-centered in our relationships. But sometimes we don't always have a clear picture. The Bible says, "Now we see but a poor reflection as in a mirror; then we shall see face to face. Now I know in part; then I shall know fully, even as I am fully known" (1 Corinthians 13:12). Our understanding of reality is often clouded. Seldom do we look through God's eyes to see how closely we sometimes resemble the narcissus, a variety of daffodil equipped with a large trumpet seemingly for tooting its own horn.

In order to have a life full of healthy, rewarding relationships, we must reflect on what the Word of God says about the selflessness of unconditional love. Perhaps the clearest picture is found in Philippians 2:3,4: "Do nothing out of selfish ambition or vain conceit, but in humility consider others better than yourselves. Each of you should look not only to your own interests, but also to the interests of others."

Notice first that the apostle Paul doesn't condemn looking after yourself and your own interests as a sin. Unconditional love doesn't mean that you only focus on others around you and forget about your own needs. Even Jesus occasionally took time apart from the needy multitudes to commune with His Father alone. Similarly, it is healthy for us to be aware of our own needs and interests and seek the Lord daily to have them met.

But notice also that the needs and interests of others are always to be a primary concern in our lives. Paul echoes this concern in Romans 12:10: "Be devoted to one another in brotherly love. Honor one another above yourselves." A key to a healthy garden of friends is to be other-centered rather than self-centered, a giver in relationships rather than a taker.

The world, however, teaches us a completely opposite goal for relationships: Put yourself first and get everything you want one way or another. The world also promotes a different strategy for relationships: Control others any way you can in order to get what you want.

People who live by these self-seeking rules are like creepy, crawly vines that climb up, tumble over, and twine themselves around other people to get to the top and achieve their selfish aims. Vine-like people are opportunists, takers in relationships. Unfortunately, such opportunism is usually unhealthy because it is inconsiderate of others.

Like honeysuckles or sweet peas, self-seekers may first appear charming and self-assured. But it is soon apparent that they are only out to overrun others in the garden. Eventually our controlling friends become difficult when they don't get their own way. Whether they know what they want or not is not the issue. The issue is who is in control.

If we are going to enjoy healthy, nurturing friendships we must recognize these tendencies toward self-centeredness in ourselves, replace them with attitudes and actions of other-centeredness, and help our friends do the same.

But how can we recognize these negative tendencies? How do creeping, vine-like people impose their self-centeredness on others? Primarily by surrounding and controlling their friends with the tendrils of manipulation, domination, and intimidation.

Self-Seeking Through Manipulation, Intimidation, and Domination

One of the ways people are tempted to control others for their own aims is through manipulation. Manipulative people resemble innocent-looking morning glories, twining themselves around their friends with "poor me" words and actions, hoping others will feel sorry for them and do what they want. When this person finds another to control, it is the typical user/used relationship. The manipulator has a full set of classic lines to keep others under control: "Why are you doing this to me? I don't deserve this"; "It's all your fault"; "Look what I have to put up with"; "Never mind. I'll take care of it"; "I can't take much more of this."

My friend Cortney is constantly allowing herself to be manipulated into taking care of her friend Fran's children. She finds herself giving in to Fran's subtle, sad-eyed hints like, "I really need help with the kids" or "Christians always talk of helping their sisters and brothers, but where are they when you need them?" Sometimes Fran is more blunt in her approach, lamenting, "I just don't know what I am going to do. I have to go out, and I have no one to watch my children."

Fran never comes right out and asks Cortney to take care of her children. She just states her need and leaves the conversation dangling. She knows Cortney is easily controlled by seeing a need and feeling obligated to fill it. By the end of the conversation Fran is happy because she has accomplished her mission of pawning off her kids on someone else. But Cortney often feels resentful and angry about being manipulated because she lacks the ability to say no. Their friendship is slowly being smothered by Fran's manipulation.

Guilt is another strategy used by self-seeking people to manipulate others to their own ends. Manipulation through guilt sometimes sounds like this: "If you really loved me you would do what I ask"; "Your attitude is not very Christ-like." They hope the guilt they inflict on others will trigger a response that fills their selfish needs.

Martyrdom, something of a cousin to guilt, is another pseudo-spiritual manipulative strategy. The self-seeking martyr says things like: "God understands me and loves me even if nobody else does. I know He'll speak to someone about helping me. Until then, I guess I'll just try to hang on." These "suffering saints" use their apparent righteousness and obedience as a lever to get others to do what they want.

People who manipulate others with guilt or martyrdom are out of touch with their own feelings and thus seldom concerned about the feelings of those they manipulate. Those who continue to manipulate their friends using tactics of guilt and martyrdom will find the life gradually being squeezed out of their relationships.

Intimidation is another controlling strategy of vine-like individuals for attempting to get their selfish needs met. Like the clematis, one of the most decorative and beautiful vines in the garden, these controlling people reach out their tendrils of intimidation and twist around vulnerable friends with a stranglehold of fear. What do intimidators sound like? They say things like:

"If you don't do what I ask, I won't be your friend"; "You'd better pay attention to what I'm telling you or else"; "How dare you question me!"; "You can't do it. There's no use trying." These messages of intimidation target a friend's fear of failure, rejection, or abandonment.

Intimidation through fear is often at the root of abuse in families as parents strive to control the behavior of their children. Unfortunately, this "do it or else" mentality can also be found in the family of God. Some Christian brothers and sisters try to intimidate others with "the fear of the Lord." They are not as concerned with God's will in the life of their friends as they are in imposing their own will in order to have their needs, wants, and desires fulfilled.

Intimidating friends often try to exert their will on others in the form of "advice." When friends offer advice free of any manipulation or intimidation, they are not offended if it is not heeded. But if the person giving the advice is obviously hurt or angry when the directives are not followed, perhaps the advice was nothing more than an attempt to control for selfish purposes. If this attempt fails, they may move to a more severe controlling strategy: domination.

A third controlling strategy is domination. Dominating individuals control their friends by attempting to cut off the influence of all other relationships. Like the climbing hydrangea with its heart-shaped leaves and creamy flowers, dominating people take on the smothering features of control.

Though they package their behavior as romantic love or sincere caring for another, dominating friends actually want all the happiness, contentment, and stability in their friend's life to depend totally on them.

"Where would so-and-so be without me?" they ask themselves. But just as a dominating vine can destroy the plants it surrounds for support, so healthy relationships will suffocate under such smothering attachment.

Growing as a Giver Instead of a Taker

Controlling others for our own benefit through manipulation, intimidation, or domination, no matter how subtle or spiritual it may appear, is not in harmony with God's call to nurture our friends with unconditional love. God's system of relating to others is that of giving with no thought of return. That's why Jesus taught, "When you give a luncheon or dinner, do not invite your friends, your brothers or relatives, or your rich neighbors; if you do, they may invite you back and so you will be repaid. But when you give a banquet, invite the poor, the crippled, the lame, the blind, and you will be blessed. Although they cannot repay you, you will be repaid at the resurrection of the righteous" (Luke 14:12-14).

Jesus was a giver, not a taker. If we want the character of Jesus to be seen in us, we will seek to grow in the grace of giving in our relationships. I have been blessed to see this grace grow in the lives of my own children. My youngest daughter Annie gave up her birthday money to help needy children, and her 12-year-old sister Katy joyfully and willingly donated her much-treasured Barbie doll and clothes to two little girls in an earthquake-devastated third world country.

One of the most important things we can give to people is our friendship—with no strings attached. Dr. Lewis Smedes writes, "A real gift costs something to give but nothing to get."[1]

We give because we have already received from God. He gave His unconditional love at the cost of His Son.

Until we replace our self-seeking tendencies with unconditional love, we will not be able to give to our friends without expecting something in return. In almost every relationship we will evaluate situations by asking, "What will I get out of this? How is this going to benefit me now or in the future?" For example, you may decide to watch the neighbor's children for the weekend, consoled by the thought that in a couple of months you and your husband may want to get away. And guess what? Your neighbor will owe you a favor. Your reasoning is, "I'm sure she will do this for me. After all, I watched her kids."

If you expect repayment of some kind down the line for what you give in friendship, then you are not giving out of love. And if your friend doesn't return the favor when you believe payment is due, and you label them inconsiderate or selfish and yourself as someone who was used, you need to ask yourself, "Who is really the selfish one?"

If you find any self-seeking tendrils of control creeping from your heart and suffocating your friends, confess them, lay them on the altar before the Lord, and forsake them. Focus your life on being a giver in your relationships, not a taker. Commit yourself to nurturing others selflessly, and you will reap the benefits of a healthy garden of friends.

Establishing Boundaries in Your Garden

At the same time, we must know how to respond positively to friends who tend to manipulate us to serve their selfish aims. Remember: Unconditional love doesn't mean you must allow others to twine their tendrils around you and control you. Like an untended vine in a garden, they will take over your life if you let them. People like my friend Cortney are easy targets for self-seeking people because they are immature in the art of holding their ground against them. They end up tolerating their controlling friends' selfish behavior and making excuses for them.

A skilled gardener knows that sometimes you have to set up boundaries in a garden to prevent a vine from taking over. And sometimes even a boundary isn't enough; shearing is necessary. Similarly, you may need to establish some boundaries and shear your vine-like friends to prevent them from taking over your life. Boundaries can be either verbal or nonverbal lines that establish what you will and will not accept in a relationship.

When I was in high school I became platonic friends with a guy who was a few years older than I. Brad and I were exact opposites. He was heavily involved in drugs; I never tried them. Brad respected the fact I chose not to experiment; I hurt for him because he was so totally consumed. I painfully watched him throw his life away. I wanted so desperately to rescue my friend from himself. He told me time and time again how much he depended on our friendship, how he was going to change if I would just be patient with him.

Finally, a conversation with my father led me to realize Brad was not going to change. I wasn't going to be able to help him because Brad did not want to be helped. By trying to control Brad's behavior, I had allowed Brad to control me. My support was nothing more than a crutch he used for sympathy.

With all my strength, I had to shear the life-draining tendrils of my clinging vine friend. I had to tell him my new limits on our relationship. I could no longer associate with him on a consistent basis until he showed real steps toward changing his lifestyle. What I felt in my heart toward Brad did not change. Only the boundaries changed.

One of the boundaries you may need to establish in relationships will distinguish between a friend's needs and expectations. As givers, we are committed to meeting genuine needs in our friends whenever it is in our power to do so. But we are not responsible to fulfill all their expectations, especially if they spring from selfish roots. Some friends expect more than we are free to give. Enough is never enough. The result: Relationships become unhealthy; friendships become twisted and distorted.

My friend Brad expected me to remain his supportive, sympathetic friend while he wallowed in his drug habit. But what he really needed, even though he didn't know it, was someone to hold him accountable for his destructive behavior. As a true friend, I could meet his need, but I could not fulfill his expectation. It was a boundary I needed to establish for Brad's good and for mine. You may face the same kinds of challenges in your friendships.

Establishing boundaries in our relationships with self-seeking friends is vital to our healthy garden. When we don't hold our friends accountable for their selfish actions, we end up tolerating their selfish behavior and making excuses for them. That's when we begin feeling like a doormat. The health of the relationship begins deteriorating because of conscious or subconscious resentment. We are angry at our friend for controlling us and using us selfishly, and we are angry at ourselves for letting it happen.

Remember, however, that our purpose in establishing boundaries and shearing invasive tendrils is not to exclude people from our lives. We simply want to encourage the development of friendships that glorify God and will be mutually enriching and rewarding at the same time.

CHAPTER ELEVEN

Don't Let Your Anger Cut Down Your Friends

One day I was cruising down a busy avenue at a fairly high speed when another car cut me off. Only by slamming on my brakes was I able to prevent the re-shaping of our fenders. Resisting the urge to lay on my horn, the words "you jerk" wanted to blast out of my mouth. At the next red light I glanced over to see what kind of person could be so inconsiderate toward another driver. Amazingly, the woman was one of my friends. When she saw me she turned beet red. Then she rolled down the window and delivered a feeble excuse for her reckless driving. I assured her it was no problem, real-izing I could be guilty of doing the same thing to some-one else some day.

My friend called me later. "You know, I was wrong. Even if you had been a stranger instead of my friend, I was wrong to cut you off like that." She couldn't believe I wasn't ready to bite her head off for such an inconsiderate stunt. In this situation, God was allowed to minister a greater understanding of love to my friend because I was able to satisfy the next condition for love on our checklist for a healthy garden: Love is not easily angered.

Actually, the phrase should read a bit differently. The translators of the original King James version must have thought a slight edit was needed to make this attribute more livable. So they added the word "easily." According to the Greek manuscripts the statement is absolute: Love is not roused to anger—period. Anger directed toward an individual is not acceptable.

The only time anger is accepted in the Bible is when it is targeted against society's sinful condition or the rejection of the gospel. The same Greek word, *paroxunomai*, translated "angered" in 1 Corinthians 13:5, is translated "distressed" in Acts 17:16: "While Paul was waiting for [Silas and Timothy] in Athens, he was greatly distressed to see that the city was full of idols." Paul's righteous indignation was acceptable because it was directed at idolatry in the Greek culture. However, even righteous anger must be kept in check. In Ephesians 4:26, which includes a quote from Psalm 4:4, Paul wrote: "In your anger do not sin: Do not let the sun go down while you are still angry."

In our garden of friends, anger is like one of those power driven weed-eaters. It was designed to slash away at the weeds that can so easily overrun a beautiful garden. But a weed-eater was never meant to be used on flowers. It will destroy them, whack them to shreds in seconds. Likewise, properly channeled righteous indignation against sin is okay, but anger directed against another person is unacceptable.

When an Angry Response Is Triggered

You may be wondering, "What's so unacceptable about anger? It seems like such a natural response." Yes, anger is a natural response. In his book, *Make Anger Your Ally*, Dr. Neil Clark Warren says that anger "is typically experienced as an almost automatic inner response to hurt, frustration, or fear."[1]

When a painful, frustrating, or frightening event triggers an angry response within us, we are physically ready to respond. Our hearts beat faster, our bodies secrete more adrenaline, our breathing increases, and our pupils dilate. All the power available inside us is primed and ready to act.

The problem with anger is not with this internal response to an event; it's what we do with it. All this power and preparedness can be dangerous. Turned on ourselves, anger can weigh us down with depression and obliterate our ability to see ourselves through God's eyes. Denied and buried inside, anger can literally bury us by prompting a heart attack or stroke. Or if we let it fly the wrong way, like a weed-eater out of control, anger can rip into some of our most cherished family members, friends, or coworkers. If we don't deal with anger in a timely manner, resentment and hostility will engulf us, and we'll be miserable to be around. What we do with anger is important to ourselves and our friends.

A high percentage of aggressive anger is expressed in machine gun bursts of cutting remarks. Dr. Warren comments:

What are these verbal explosions all about? They're almost always about unmet needs—needs to feel complete or perfect or secure.... If you find your-self exploding regularly at someone, ask yourself what needs you think that person is failing to meet for you. That someone may be your spouse, friend, co-worker, opponent, or God Himself. It doesn't matter. Our explosive anger still relates to an un-met need.

Sometimes we have an unconscious need to be seen as perfect. Social approval becomes like a god for us. And we seem to assume that approval re-quires perfection. Since criticism indicates flaw, and flaw jeopardizes approval, we explode in re-sponse to the slightest critical remark about us. Criticism threatens our fragile psychic structures, which depend on our ability to gain others' ap-proval by being good enough.[2]

Though we may think it is better to let our anger out explosively, the satisfaction is only short-term. Instead of reaping the love and appreciation of our friends for our "honest expression," we gain only their disrespect and resentment, whether they reflect it openly or harbor it secretly, for the pain we cause.

On the other hand, secret or subtle anger is some-times so cleverly disguised even we don't recognize it for what it is. We only see the wide path of de-struction left behind in our gardens after we have coldly cut through a relationship. We must keep an eye out for covert as well as overt expressions of anger.

Expressing Anger Is Your Choice

Dr. Warren continues,

When we *do* something with our anger, we have
moved to anger expression. And *how* we express
our anger is learned. Nothing about it is inherited.
Thus, that expression can be modified.[3]

Regardless of how you have expressed your anger previously, you can change that pattern of behavior.

Whenever the friends in your garden provoke an
angry response in you, let your first response be to pray
to God the words of Solomon, "Catch for us the foxes,
the little foxes that ruin the vineyards, our vineyards
that are in bloom" (Song of Songs 2:15). Uncontrolled
anger is like foxes loose in the garden. If they're not
caught and contained, they'll eat all the grapes and
spoil the harvest. Similarly, we need to seek the Lord
first and rely on His wisdom and strength to keep us
from ripping into our friends like a weed-eater in the
flower bed.

Next, evaluate your feelings and take time to
think before you react. It is important to try to delay
any expression of your anger until you've had a chance
to think through just what you are trying to accomplish.
Learn to ask yourself these questions:

1. Why am I angry? Remember: Anger is usually
prompted by pain, frustration, or fear. Are you angry
because someone hurt you, frustrated you, or fright-
ened you in some way? Who was it? What did they do?

When my friend cut me off, my anger was the
result of fear. Her thoughtlessness could have caused a
serious accident. At other times my anger has been
prompted by hurt, as it was when Susan called to confront me about the negative aspects of my personality
(see Chapter 6). I was further angered by the frustration
I felt when Susan informed me about others I had hurt

but refused to tell me their names so I could apologize to them.

2. What needs to happen in this encounter to ensure the long-term relationship I want to have with this person? In others words, what's the best thing that could happen in the anger-producing situation that will allow you and your friend to remain friends?

Sitting across from my friend at the red light, I knew if I expressed my anger negatively I could damage our friendship. That's not what I wanted. The best thing that could happen for our relationship at that point was for me to lovingly express my understanding and allow God to convict her heart. In the incident with Susan, the best thing I could do for our relationship was to work through my anger without letting her know how I felt.

3. How can I help the best happen? That is, what will be your strategy for resolving your angry feelings without mowing down your friend?

The strategy I used at the stoplight for resolving my fear-induced anger and maintaining my relationship was to empathize with my embarrassed friend, knowing that I am perfectly capable of thoughtlessness on the highway myself. With Susan, I resolved my anger by looking for new ways to express my love and friendship to her despite my hurt. Examining our friendship by writing down my thoughts helped me to get a clearer picture of those new avenues of expression.

This third question needs to take into consideration several crucial variables: the personalities of the people involved; your relationship to these people; the amount of time available; the amount of time invested; the constraints defining the situation.[4]

This is where knowing a person's background helps you understand where they're coming from, their thinking process. According to Dr. Warren, studies show that when we can identify with the person with whom we're angry, our preparedness to react dissipates significantly.

Taking into consideration all these factors, we must not stop there. The key to keeping anger from destroying our friendships is implementing our well-thought-out, prayed-for strategy. "Not to carry out your strategy will leave you with unresolved hurt, frustration, and fear. It will also increase the chances that your anger experience will return—the next time it will be much more difficult to handle."[5]

By putting our strategies into action, we start the process of learning how to express our anger constructively. This requires thinking. We can choose our method of expression. We can choose to mimic the character of Jesus in our response to those who anger us. The end result of our self-discipline is most rewarding. We exchange destructive anger for health and growth in our friendships. Then we can identify with Solomon when he wrote, "See! The winter is past; the rains are over and gone. Flowers appear on the earth; the season of singing has come" (Song of Songs 2:11,12).

CHAPTER TWELVE

Prune Away the Dead Leaves of Yesterday

My friend Beverly has four sisters. One day Beverly's mother telephoned her, torn by anger and hurt. She had just received a stinging letter from another daughter who viciously accused her of favoring Beverly over her other girls. The angry daughter claimed the only thing she ever had in common with her mother was the umbilical cord. The words cut her mother deeply.

Beverly and the other three sisters tried to console their mother. Yet they grieved over the chasm that now existed in the family. The sister who had written the letter displayed no remorse. Her mother believed the relationship with her resentful daughter could never be the same. Beverly despaired that her mother would never take steps to restore the family relationship.

About a week later Beverly's mother informed

her that she had forgiven her distraught daughter. To prove it she sent her a love letter. My friend was very relieved, believing God could now start a true healing process in her family.

Beverly saw the sending of this note of affection as a direct result of her mother following the next condition on our checklist for maintaining healthy relationships: Love keeps no record of wrongs. In other words, love "does not reckon up or calculatingly consider the evil done to it."[1]

It means slipping on our gloves of compassion and tenderly trimming away the yellow leaves and decayed stems of the offenses of the past.

But how do we do this? We use the pruning shears of forgiveness designed to enhance the beauty of our garden of friends. The shears of forgiveness are equipped with a pair of sharp blades. When these two blades come together in godly precision, a healthy cut of forgiveness is made and the pain of offense falls away.

One of the blades of forgiveness is the decision to let go of the wrong you suffered. This is the way God treats our offenses. He said in the book of Isaiah, "I, even I, am he who blots out your transgressions, for my own sake, and remembers your sins no more" (43:25). Some people take this verse to mean God literally forgets our sins. Others say that an all-knowing God can't forget anything, and that references to God "forgetting" our sin are figurative of His act of totally separating Himself from our confessed and forgiven sin. Either way, it's comforting to know that when God forgives us He lets go of our sin and never holds it against us. And since He commands us in His Word to forgive others as He has forgiven us (Matthew 6:12,14,15; Colossians 3:13), we must also let go of the hurtful things people do to us.

How do we know if we have let go of a friend's offense? Have you ever thought or said, "I've forgiven him, but I'll never forget what he did to me"? If so, you probably haven't let go of the offense, because you frequently rehearse the wrong in your mind and with others so no detail is lost over time. You're probably not walking in true forgiveness because you're holding on to something God wants you to let go of.

Forgiving is not the same as forgetting. But when you truly let go of an offense, in time you'll be able to think about and even be with the person who offended you without feeling the pain, anger, or resentment. But if you say "I forgive" but continue to think about every detail of what happened, you haven't really forgiven.

The other blade of forgiveness is the decision to never again hold your friend accountable for his or her wrong. This aspect of God's forgiveness is pictured in Psalm 103:12: "As far as the east is from the west, so far has he removed our transgressions from us." God not only let go of our sins, He threw them as far away as possible. He didn't keep them in a drawer nearby to pull out and use against us in the future. Similarly, when we prune away a friend's offense by letting go of it, we must also carry it to the burn pile and leave it there. Once you do this, you never bring it up again in your conversation as a weapon against the offender. It's as if the wrong never happened in your relationship.

As it turned out, Beverly's mother never completely let go of or separated herself from her daughter's offense. Six months later Beverly discovered that her mother had kept her daughter's hateful letter. When asked why, she answered, "Just in case she ever denies what she said to me, I'll have proof of it in black and white."

Snapshots from the Past

Sometimes the record of wrongs we hold against our friends is a mental snapshot instead of a poison pen letter. This was true in my relationship with George, a friend of my husband.

In the early days of our marriage, Rich and I had differing perspectives about George. Rich's friend seemed like a good Christian man. But whenever the three of us were together, warning bells went off inside me. Something about George concerned me. But when I mentioned it to Rich, he told me not to worry and assured me that George was fine. Rich continued to invest time and energy in George, and I continued to anticipate trouble.

Over the next two years my concern was justified. It seemed that George wasn't as spiritual as he wanted us to believe. He had an affair, deserted his family, married another woman, and moved out of state. Our differences in perspective over George left a wedge between Rich and me that took a considerable amount of time to heal. And as much as I tried to forgive George for his dishonesty to us, just hearing his name made me cringe.

Over time both the memory and pain of George's offense seemed to fade. Then one day a fellowship group was meeting in our home. While all of us were worshiping and praying, suddenly there was a tap on my shoulder. Turning around, I could hardly believe my eyes. There, standing in my living room, was George. What audacity! All I could think about was how he had taken advantage of Rich in the past. Surely he was back to do it again. Despite the spiritual atmosphere of love and praise in our home at that moment, all my emotions came rushing to the surface. With a few carefully chosen, pointed words directed at my husband, I stormed outside.

Right behind me followed my gentle and wise friend Jill. I poured out to her all that happened in the past and my fears of a repeat performance. I was sure this guy was going to deceive Rich again. But Jill exhorted me to remember that Rich had experienced tremendous spiritual growth since he'd last seen George. Rich would know how to respond to him.

Jill also reminded me that I had grown a lot spiritually, even though I knew I wasn't displaying it at the moment. "If I'm different, why did I react toward George the way I did?" I asked.

Jill explained that I had taken a mental snapshot years ago of George and Rich's relationship. When George walked through the door, instead of seeing my husband for the new man he had become, I pulled out the old picture and said, "It's going to happen all over again. George is still the same conniver he was years ago. Rich is still the same gullible person with the same reactions. George can still deceive Rich."

Jill pointed out this was sin in my life. I had no right to hold Rich to his old way of thinking or behaving. I was refusing to acknowledge the growth he had experienced.

I had also confined my view of George to the old snapshot of him in my mind. It was as if none of us had grown, changed, or advanced at all. My spiritual immaturity fit the old picture perfectly. My reaction proved I had developed that old photograph in the caustic combination of bitterness and unforgiveness. I realized I had only deceived myself into believing I had forgiven George. I actually detested him from long distance. If I had examined myself honestly during George's absence,

I would have known this was true. There were definite warning signs, like cringing whenever I heard his name.

Sometimes you believe you have forgiven a friend for something he or she has done—until it happens a second or third time. Suddenly, you feel a little jab of anger inside, and you start to feel the previous hurt all over again. Roots of bitterness are revealed when our reactions are inappropriate in a particular incident. When that happens, stop where you are. Just say, "God, so-and-so hurt me when he did such-and-such. Don't hold it to his account. I choose to forgive him. I pray that this root of bitterness in me will die so it can't hurt me anymore."

George didn't stay around for long. After talking to him, it was obvious he hadn't changed. But after Jill's exhortation and a time of heart-searching prayer, I changed. For the first time, my heart grieved for George. No longer looking at him from my perspective, I saw him through God's eyes and freely forgave him.

Caring Enough to Confront

Forgiveness must be extended even if those who hurt us don't ask for it. True, when others wrong us it is their responsibility to come to us and ask for forgiveness; we're not required to go to them and tell them they have offended us (Matthew 5:23,24). But whether they come to us or not, we still need to forgive them. Only when we have forgiven those who hurt us are we in a position to be a friend to them. By the same token, when you hurt someone, you are responsible to go and ask for forgiveness once you have confessed your sin to God. Asking forgiveness of a friend is crucial to maintaining a harmonious relationship with God.

After you have chosen to forgive, God may have you talk to your friends about their behavior. The focus of this confrontation should not be how their behavior has hurt you but how it is hurting them. If you want to talk to them in order to vent your feelings or set them straight, you're confronting for the wrong reasons, so avoid it.

If you find yourself in a friendship where you are constantly hurting one another or there is repetitive behavior that bothers you, you need to address the situation. Go to this person and tell him or her your feelings. In the pruning process, it is better to expose these wounds to the air. If they are painted over with the protective covering of denial, disease may grow beneath the surface. The only acceptable treatment for continuing conflict is the healing medicine of God's unconditional love expressed through loving confrontation.

But be careful not to attack a friend by saying, "You always do this." By doing so we fail to allow ourselves the chance to recognize any positive changes in the other person. Instead we need to approach each other on the level of exposing our own hearts rather than confronting a friend's actions. Let your friend know, "When we have these conversations, I feel inadequate" or "My feelings get hurt because I don't understand." Take the "me" or "I" approach of explaining what happens inside you instead of making "you" accusations.

Then ask, "Is there some way we can deal with this differently?" In doing so you are letting your friend know the relationship can't continue at its present level. You are setting a boundary in terms of the relationship, not in terms of his or her behavior. In essence you are saying, "This is not acceptable in our relationship. But I'm willing to work with you toward a solution that will be good for our friendship."

Once you have pruned away the dead leaves of an offense through loving forgiveness, what happens to the relationship? In some cases, if the pain is minor and the fellowship has been restored, the friendship may pick up right where it left off. There are other times when it is healthier to keep some distance in the friendship instead of forcing the relationship to its former closeness right away. Allowing space for a friendship to lie dormant in our garden may keep us from uprooting our friend entirely.

But distance between friends should not be maintained as a form of punishment by withdrawing our love or forgetting about them. We should send a note occasionally or let them know through other people that we still care. Make sure any words you speak about them are positive. Under these conditions, the friendship can endure the separation and blossom again.

When a Friendship Doesn't Heal

There are times friendships do not survive a hurt suffered even when forgiveness has been extended to the offenders. When a friendship is uprooted, you may question your ability to care: "God, what did I do wrong? Why was this person in my life for this time? Why did this person leave my life? Do I have a brown thumb when it comes to cultivating healthy friendships?"

God doesn't always answer our questions regarding why a relationship dies in our life. But the Lord taught me a lesson about failed relationships through the parable of the farmer sowing seed in Matthew 13:3-8, 18-23. Jesus taught that the seed sown is God's Word, and the different soils represent how people respond, or fail to respond, to the Word sown in their hearts.

The story has a parallel in how we cultivate relationships and how friendships respond to hurt. In some people the seed of friendship flourishes productively. But some friendships die due to misunderstanding. Others lack the commitment necessary to go through hard times. And others fail because a friend values wealth and other things more than your friendship. Even when a friendship dies a painful death we are called to live in forgiveness and unconditional love toward our former friend. There are times when we must bless a friend by allowing them to leave our gardens and continue on their journey through life without us.

God taught us this lesson through a couple he brought into our lives named Lloyd and Anna. Right after we met, this young couple asked Rich and I to teach them godly principles for their lives. Lloyd desperately needed direction for handling his business. His mismanagement had landed them deeply in debt. And Anna was adjusting to her new role as a wife. They wanted to live in the greenhouse of our garden where we could bring some stability to their lives.

Because we felt this was something God wanted us to do, we entered into a very intense period of devoting our time and energy to Lloyd and Anna. We knew in the beginning that the relationship would be one-sided. We would be doing all the nurturing and giving. There were months of business meetings, phone calls, visiting, sharing meals in our home, and monetary assistance to help relieve their financial pressure. Sometimes Rich and I felt we were helping them too much. Perhaps our assistance was more like a comfortable nursery for our friends instead of an encouragement to grow into Christian maturity. But we weren't sure.

As Lloyd and Anna began to mature we felt it was no longer necessary to hover over them so closely. It was time to transplant them from the greenhouse into our garden and begin redefining our relationship from the discipling role to a more balanced friendship. But Lloyd and Anna preferred the original relationship because it did not require anything of them. They were like children who didn't want to grow up. The only time we heard from them was when they needed something.

Word got back to us that Lloyd and Anna used our names on numerous occasions to open doors of personal opportunity with other people. Furthermore, after all we had done for them and given them, Lloyd turned around and tried to take advantage of Philip, a mutual friend. Lloyd offered to do some work for Philip's ministry, then demanded payment for work Philip had not authorized.

At Lloyd's request we intervened in the matter. It was obvious that Lloyd was in the wrong. We challenged him to release Philip from any obligation for payment just as we had released Lloyd from paying us for all we had done for him and Anna. Lloyd begrudgingly gave in. After that night we never heard from Lloyd again. Finally, having exhausted all their resources in Southern California, Lloyd and Anna moved to Nashville, Tennessee.

Lloyd and Anna totally discarded our friendship. It no longer benefited them. Actually, there never really was a friendship on their part. It was only the appearance of one. The reality of this hurt us deeply. We felt manipulated, unappreciated, and used.

Rich and I went through a time of grieving. We grieved because our expectations were not met, especially the expectation of a long-term friendship. We wanted to see some positive changes in Lloyd and Anna after having poured so much of our time, energy, and money into our tender friends. The only visible fruits of our labor were that they were no longer in debt and they had better business sense. We were grieved that our friendship had not developed.

Rich and I turned to God for comfort, and with His help we were able to see beyond the hurt. We were able to get past our emotions. We sat down together and repented of any hardness in our hearts. We shared the depth of our hurt and disappointment with each other alone. Together we forgave Lloyd and Anna for hurting us. We snipped away the dead leaves of the past and threw them away.

After two years of an intense discipling relationship with Lloyd and Anna, Rich and I needed to minimize our sorrow by filling the gap left by our departing friends. We turned to God for His wisdom. We claimed God's promise: "I will turn their mourning into gladness; I will give them comfort and joy instead of sorrow" (Jeremiah 31:13). We experienced God's comfort and joy as we laid our feelings at God's altar and interceded for our young friends, who chose not to add their beauty to our garden.

It is during the time of grieving over a lost relationship that we can experience the most spiritual growth. If you pray and patiently wait for an answer, the Lord will reveal to you how to fill the gap when someone is uprooted from your garden. He may want you to spend longer periods of intimate time with Him. Maybe He has a new set of friends He wants to bring into your life. Or perhaps you are to enjoy more family time. Patiently give God that open time, and He will

give you direction for your life that you may have previously missed. It will be a valuable time in your relationship with God and others.

We sincerely prayed, "God bless Lloyd and
Anna. Use what we have instilled in their lives over the
years, especially the real love we have for them. Help
them to see how they can duplicate this love for someone else. Do not let Your Word become void in their
lives. And leave our hearts open for them to be able to
come back."

Rich and I knew it was our responsibility to speak
blessings on Lloyd and Anna (Matthew 5:44; James 3:9,
10). And that responsibility was occasionally tested.
When other friends asked if we had heard from Lloyd
and Anna, old memories were stirred. But we never
spoke negatively of them. None of our other friends
knew anything about our pain or disappointment. We
only spoke positive words about Lloyd and Anna.

To prevent bitterness from creeping back into our
hearts, Rich and I recalled the good times we had with
Lloyd and Anna. We determined we would no longer
mention anything negative that happened between the
four of us. God wanted us to have sweet memories of
Lloyd and Anna and to share positive things with people
who asked about them.

After a year of pondering only good memories,
Rich and I went to Nashville on a business trip. On
Sunday morning we found ourselves visiting one of the
local churches. Who did we run into? Lloyd and Anna.
We were thrilled to see the tender flowers who had
once flourished in our garden's greenhouse. We were
genuinely blessed at our reunion. But they were obviously mortified. We talked for five brief minutes, then
they completely disappeared. Rich and I just stood there

praising God. We had been walking in total forgiveness and were free to accept Lloyd and Anna just the way they were.

Unconditional Forgiveness

We initiated forgiveness toward Lloyd and Anna without it being sought. Forgiving someone without that person apologizing first was one of the hardest aspects of forgiveness I had to learn. But that's what Jesus did as He hung on the cross. He forgave us long before we confessed our sin (Romans 5:8). We must follow His example.

Forgiveness is a matter of the will, not the emotions. Jesus didn't tell us to love one another or forgive one another when we feel like it. He *commanded* us to love and forgive one another—period. When we choose to forgive even when we don't feel forgiving, we are choosing to obey God. Forgive obediently, and the feelings of forgiveness will eventually follow.

Jesus taught us to pray, "Forgive us our debts, as we also have forgiven our debtors" (Matthew 6:12). What was Jesus saying? "Forgive us for failing to love others, as we also have forgiven others who have failed to love us." Unconditional love is the only debt we owe. Paul emphasized this fact in his letter to the Romans: "Owe no one anything except to love one another" (13:8, NKJV).

Unconditional love and forgiveness know no limits. Peter asked Jesus, "Lord, how many times shall I forgive my brother when he sins against me? Up to seven times?" (Matthew 18:21). He probably thought seven times was being generous. But Jesus answered, "Not seven times, but seventy-seven times" (v. 22).

Jesus was declaring that forgiveness is a matter of attitude, not mathematics.[2]

It is always easier to forgive someone if we can put ourselves in their place, slip into their shoes. In pruning, the gardener needs to understand the growing habits of each flower in their garden. Similarly, we need to empathize with the person who has wronged us. Dr. Neil Clark Warren believes the two prerequisites to learning empathy skills are: "You must genuinely want to understand the other person" and "you must be patient—willing to allow persons to reveal themselves gradually and in their own time."

He goes on to say, "No path to forgiveness is straighter or truer than understanding. Learning how to be empathetic and then practicing that skill can alter your way of relating to others significantly. It is a quality well worth the effort required to develop it."[3]

Are you clinging to any dead leaves of the past in your relationships with your friends? If so, it's time to get out the shears of forgiveness and start snipping.

CHAPTER THIRTEEN

Get Rid of the Pests of Negative Thinking

One of the greatest dangers to a healthy garden is the unhindered invasion of creepy, crawly pests that bore and chew their way through roots, leaves, stems, and flowers. Aphids and cutworms, slugs and snails will slowly but surely turn a beautiful garden into a wasteland unless they are detected and destroyed.

The garden of our lives is threatened by a similar subtle invasion. It's the destructive attitude suggested in our next attribute of love: Love does not delight in evil but rejoices with the truth. Paul implies that we can join one of two cheering sections with regard to the friends in our garden. One section cheers when something evil or negative happens in a friend's life. The other section rejoices in the good, positive things that happen to others. These responses are first attitudes that we hold toward others. But like any attitude, your positivism or negativism will eventually become actions that will either nurture your garden of friends or decimate it.

The Danger of Delighting in Evil

Unconditional love doesn't delight in the negative things that happen to others. The cheerleaders in this section are envy, pride, selfishness, and revenge. They urge us to applaud any misfortune or failure our friends suffer because their negative circumstances make us look good or feel vindicated. They deceive us into thinking our unfortunate friends deserve what they get. Like unwanted pests in a garden, delighting in the negative experiences of others will eventually eat away at the beauty of your garden of friends.

Many times I have seen people derive a sense of comfort from negative events experienced by a friend or coworker who has not met their expectations or has treated them unfairly. Kathy's husband Joe worked for a big defense contractor. His boss, Mark, was a ruthlessly dishonest man who destroyed Joe's reputation in the industry through a series of lies about him. Joe hasn't been able to find employment in his field of expertise because of Mark's far-reaching influence in the industry.

Joe and Kathy's frustration and disappointment recruited them for the negative cheering section. Every time Joe's former employer lost a government contract or received bad press, the couple took comfort in the fact that Mark and the company were getting what they deserved. "You can't treat people like they treated us and get away with it," they agreed.

Joe and Kathy thought their attitude was perfectly acceptable to God until they read in Proverbs 24:17,18: "Do not gloat when your enemy falls; when he stumbles, do not let your heart rejoice, or the Lord will see and disapprove and turn his wrath away from him." They discovered an important truth for their relationships. Even when God brings His vengeance or judgment on someone, He wants us in the right cheering section. As Obadiah verses 12 and 15 say, "You should not look down on your brother in the day of his misfortune, nor rejoice over the people of Judah in the day of their destruction, nor boast so much in the day of their trouble. . . . The day of the Lord is near for all nations. As you have done, it will be done to you; your deeds will return upon your own head."

What are some misfortunes others experience that tempt us to delight instead of respond with concern and prayer? Perhaps some of the following sound uncomfortably familiar:

• Your least favorite Christian television personality is accused of moral or financial impropriety. Are you tempted to say something like, "I'm glad he was found out. I hope they kick him off the air"?

• You have church friends who are more permissive in parenting than you are. Their children are continually getting in trouble in Sunday school while yours receive prizes for good behavior. Do you find yourself gloating, "It serves them right. They wouldn't listen to me when I told them to be more strict with their children"?

• The candidate you voted against for an elected church position loses the election. Do you cheer as loudly about his defeat as you do about your candidate's victory?

• You have a friendly argument with your spouse or child about a certain fact. When you are proven right, are you tempted to flaunt your "superior knowledge" in front of him or her?

If any of these responses describe you, you may be in the wrong cheering section. Delighting in the misfortune of others is a sure way to drive them out of your garden.

The Benefit of Rejoicing in Good

The right cheering section cheers excitedly when good, positive things happen to others. The captain of this cheering section is unconditional love. Love can rejoice in the good fortune and success of others because its qualities are kindness, patience, encouragement, humility, and forgiveness. Paul suggests that when our friendships are marked by unconditional love, we will always be in the cheering section that rejoices in truthful, positive experiences in their lives.

How do we make sure we're in the right cheering section? Paul gives us the key to fulfilling this love attribute in his letter to the Philippians: "Finally, brothers, whatever is true, whatever is noble, whatever is right, whatever is pure, whatever is lovely, whatever is admirable—if anything is excellent or praiseworthy—think about such things" (4:8). We are instructed to practice occupying our minds with good, positive things and stop concentrating on the negative. This instruction is just as appropriate and applicable to how we think about and relate to our friends as any other area of our lives. Once you train yourself to look for and focus on the good in your relationships, you will find it easy to join the right cheering section.

God can help you develop this positive mind-set toward others even when their negative traits may be obvious. Though my mother was manic depressive after I turned 12 years old, the Lord often reminds me of the organizational skills she taught me before her illness began. Thanks to my mom, I use my time more efficiently today.

Let God show you how the negative things in your relationships can be used for good. You will start seeing people differently and nurture your garden of friends and relationships. For example:

• Instead of rejoicing in a Christian television personality's failure, think about all the people who have been ministered to by this individual despite his weaknesses. Thank God that He can use the individual's failure to humble him, cleanse him, and prepare him for another area of ministry. Pray for this individual and consider writing him a letter encouraging him to hold fast to God and His Word in his time of failure, guilt, and restoration.

• Your friends with misbehaving children are probably really hurting. Instead of gloating in your success, empathize with their failure, because even you have failed at times as a parent. Consider writing, calling, or visiting the parents and complimenting them on the positive parenting traits they do exercise.

• You may be glad your candidate was elected to fill a significant role in the church. But think the best about the person who lost. She is also a gifted member in the body of Christ. God has placed her in the local congregation to be a blessing to you and placed you there to be a blessing to her as you exercise your gifts and serve one another. Pray that God will guide her to the exact place of ministry He has chosen for her.

• Winning an argument with a family member is no reason to exult. You'll be wrong sometimes too. Instead, rejoice in your family relationship and be thankful for the positive input they bring to your life.

Developing healthy relationships in life is a matter of focus. Do you concentrate on the bad or delight in the good? Love is always a choice. This is true in our responses to close friends, family members, strangers, or suspected enemies. You cannot be forced to love unconditionally. You cannot be forced to act unselfishly or have a positive attitude toward the flowers planted in your garden. It is your choice. And how you choose will determine whether your garden will flourish with rich relationships or be eaten away by the creepy, crawly pests of negative thinking, speaking, and acting.

CHAPTER FOURTEEN

Keep Your Friends Covered

Warm spring sunshine is a welcome, necessary ingredient in the growth of most garden plants. But blazing, ground-parching summer heat is another matter. Many flowers will wither and die in the blistering sun unless the gardener shelters the garden from the life-draining heat.

As loving caretakers in our garden of friends, we must anticipate the scorching times of trials in their lives and fulfill the next scriptural condition of love for maintaining a healthy garden: Love always protects. The Greek word, *stego*, means to "protect or preserve by covering."[1] When the searing heat of life's difficulties threatens the health and growth of our garden of friends, we need to lovingly provide the shelter they need.

Solomon wrote, "A friend loves at all times" (Proverbs 17:17) and "There is a friend who sticks closer than a brother" (Proverbs 18:24). These verses remind us that our commitment to nurture and protect our friends is for all seasons, good and bad, and is even deeper than family commitment. This latter idea contradicts the old cliché, "Blood is thicker than water," which suggests loyalty between blood relatives is stronger than between unrelated friends. Actually, our old cliché is the opposite of the original ancient saying. In some Middle Eastern cultures the wording is, "Blood is thicker than milk," referring to a covenantal blood-brother relationship. In essence it means "a person who is covenanted to you will stick by you when those born in your own family will not."[2] That's exactly what Solomon meant in Proverbs 18:24.

Jesus is the ultimate example of a friend who stays by our side through the seasonal droughts of our lives. He loved us and gave His life for us when we were in the worst shape possible: lost in sin (Romans 5:8). As children of God, we are to reflect the same unconditional love and support to the friends in our gardens. It is our expression of love for others during the difficult times of life that will cause people to know we are Christians (John 13:34,35). Why? Because many "friends" in the world today are only "fair-weather friends." When a heat wave of trials rushes in, these friends rush out. Friends who are committed to each other "at all times" reflect Christ's unconditional love.

Shelter from the Material Drought

One of the first types of protective covering we may be called on to offer friends is that of physical and financial support. The need for this type of shelter often arises suddenly and sometimes tragically.

Several years ago our friend Keith Green was killed in a plane crash with two of his children. Rich immediately offered his support by helping Keith's wife Melody and Last Days Ministries take care of the bleak, business side of death: certificates, taxes, and all the other formal documentation.

In addition to Keith's death, there was another reality facing our newly widowed friend Melody. A week prior to the accident Melody learned she was pregnant. There she was, left in charge of a large ministry with a baby daughter and pregnant with another child. Her pain was almost unbearable.

We offered Melody the shelter of our friendship. She spent the first Christmas after the tragic accident with us in California. Later Melody asked me to be her birth coach. What an honor! This required me to go to Texas and stay two weeks before the baby was born. But it was support I was eager to provide. Through the years since Keith's death, Rich and I have continued to anticipate areas where we can support Melody.

However, there have been other friends for whom we have hastily constructed a protective physical or material shelter without checking with God first. We raced to their aid at the first signs of withering without realizing God was allowing the blistering time of testing to force the taproots of our young friends to search out and drink the deeper waters of faith. By rushing in too soon we were robbing our friends of the spiritual growth God intended them to experience through the trial.

Yet sometimes Rich and I just assumed providing protective financial support in certain situations was the Christian thing to do. So we went ahead and gave our friends money and then got a strong reprimand from God for getting in His way. God had allowed the need in our friends' lives to get their attention when every other approach had been ignored.

When your friends choose to avoid God's instruction and suffer the physical or material consequences, your support role is simple: Love them through it, but don't rescue them from it. "The Lord disciplines those he loves" (Hebrews 12:6), and untimely rescuing on your part may interfere with God's loving discipline in your friend's life.

The Ministry of Prayer Support

Instead of offering physical and material relief to friends in trial, sometimes you can provide support best by praying for them. But don't confine your prayer to close friends who are hurting. Offer your protective prayer covering to anyone the Lord brings across your path who is enduring one of life's staggering heat waves.

Burt was a man with whom Rich and I have literally a passing acquaintance. We pass each other every year at the Christian Bookseller's Association convention, pausing to chat briefly and exchange the usual pleasantries. This has been the extent of our relationship for several years.

But a couple of years ago, Burt looked particularly down when we greeted him at the convention. The Lord encouraged Rich and I to let Burt know we were concerned. That was all he needed. Burt unloaded the pain of his backslidden son's crumbling marriage. This sensitive time of sharing reminded us of Isaiah's words: "The Sovereign Lord has given me an instructed tongue, to know the word that sustains the weary. He wakens me morning by morning, wakens my ear to listen like one being taught" (Isaiah 50:4).

Rich and I explained to Burt that we pray together every morning over a list of people and needs. Burt asked if his son Matthew and daughter-in-law Helen could be added to our list. We promised to pray faithfully every day until our paths crossed again the following year.

Sometime during the year, a mutual friend got word to us that Matthew and Helen had recommitted their lives to the Lord and their marriage was mending wonderfully. We rejoiced and continued to pray.

Finally convention time arrived. When we found Burt on the convention floor, we were met by someone who had experienced the transforming power of prayer. Burt introduced us to his wife who quickly produced pictures of a happy Matthew and Helen.

Though Burt and his wife would not be considered our close friends, we have a heart tie that can only come from sharing the same burden. How grateful they were that we had joined others and dedicated time to pray for their family. But the blessing to us was twofold. Praying for others is a faith builder in our own lives, and the appreciation they showed meant the world to us.

Christians tend to take too lightly their responsibility to pray for each other. Responsibility is a word we seldom relate to friendship. Responsibility requires some type of follow-through. Too many times we will say, "Sure, I will pray," when in reality our promise is nothing more than a polite response or the right thing to say. Once our friends are out of sight, our verbal commitment is out of mind. If we have no intention of praying for them in the future, we shouldn't say we will. Perhaps we should fulfill our responsibility by praying for them on the spot instead of making a false commitment.

When we give our word to pray, we need to write down the request. We also need to indicate how long we will pray for the need. If we say, "I'll pray," without attaching some type of time frame, we may tend to pray one or two Band-Aid prayers and let it go at that. This half-hearted commitment may ease our conscience, but it falls short of a responsible commitment to support a brother or sister in prayer for a month, a year, or until God brings a solution.

We have similar responsibilities when we ask our friends to support us in prayer. Many of us forget to get back to those people who are praying and let them know how God is answering prayer. We are so used to people not taking our requests for prayer to heart. How many times have we just thrown our prayer needs out in front of our friends, expecting no one to pick them up? Because our expectations are so low, we fail to report God's answer unless something great and miraculous happens.

Instead, jot down the names of the people you have asked to pray for a specific need. We need to remember to thank those people who have sincerely prayed, taking us into their hearts for a certain amount of time. Appreciation is so essential in healthy relationships. Besides, showing appreciation confirms to our friends they did something worthwhile and encourages them to do so again.

I am so grateful Jesus takes His role as intercessor for us seriously. Our commitment to pray for others should be modeled after Jesus' commitment to intercede for us before the Father (Romans 8:34). Intercession means to approach God and seek His presence and hearing on behalf of others. When we feel we have nothing to offer our friends to help them endure life's searing droughts, intercession is one of the most powerful acts of love we can provide.

According to Dr. C. Peter Wagner, Professor of Church Growth at Fuller Theological Seminary in Pasadena, California, over 85 percent of the ministries and churches that are actively supported by intercessors have noticed marked improvement or growth. They attribute this difference primarily to prayer.[3]

A Commitment to Love Proactively

Of course, our prayers and other types of protective covering should not be reserved only for our friends and acquaintances. We are to play the role of the Good Samaritan by surrounding strangers and even our enemies with our loving care. Quoting Proverbs 25:21,22, Paul wrote, "If your enemy is hungry, feed him; if he is thirsty, give him something to drink. In doing this, you will heap burning coals on his head" (Romans 12:20).

Many commentators interpret this Scripture to mean our kindness will cause embarrassment or discomfort to our enemies. Actually, it means just the opposite. In ancient cultures, if a person's fire went out, he would either have to labor to start another fire or borrow live coals from his neighbor. These coals were most likely transported on the head in some type of basket. In this sense, anyone who poured live coals on your head was doing you a great favor, providing life-sustaining fire by which you could receive warmth and cook your food.[4] Meeting the needs of friends, strangers, and enemies alike is a life-giving expression of unconditional love.

Protective, need-meeting love must be proactive. We should be looking for ways to minister to our friends in the heat of their trial. If we find ourselves too busy to offer the physical or spiritual protection necessary to our suffering friends, then we need to reexamine our schedules. Busy friends often say, "I care," but there are no actions to prove it. Love without actions is rather empty.

Sometimes busy people try to escape their responsibility to friendships by saying the right words, like "Just trust the Lord" or "God will provide." These words are empty unless we take time to find out what our friends are going through and how they really feel. We need to hear their hurt and feel their pain. This will help us know how best to supply a protective covering. A pat answer will never replace a genuine hug. And saying "be warmed and filled" is no substitute for providing the needs of a hurting friend (James 2:15,16).

Caring takes a degree of commitment on our part, because commitment is a step beyond what is necessary or expected. But when we have expressed our commitment to protect our friends in their difficult trials, we have a responsibility to fulfill that commitment. This is how we begin to build trust in our relationships.

CHAPTER FIFTEEN

Nourish Hearts with Hope and Faith

Look around your garden of friends. Do any of them seem to be dying on the vine, sort of withering away before your very eyes? Are they a little yellow around the edges from the cares and difficulties of life? Are their smiles few and far between? Maybe yesterday's challenges have turned into today's burdens. Perhaps life has left them limp with depression.

If you find any of your friends in this condition, I guarantee they are lacking at least one of the next two attributes listed in 1 Corinthians 13: Love always trusts, love always hopes. I call these two conditions God's prescription for fruitfulness. Even though Paul lists trust before hope in this checklist, hope must always precede faith in practical application, so we will consider them in this order.

Being a Hope-filled Friend

Hope means positively expecting to obtain something. Unconditional love in your friendships should spark a mutual, positive expectancy for life. Biblical hope is filled with encouragement and devoid of disappointment (Romans 5:5). *Hope does not dissapoint, because the love of God has been poured out within our hearts, through the Holy Spirit who was given to us.*

So why do we sometimes find ourselves or our friends drooping in disappointment or despair? Because we place our hope in people and material things instead of the promises of God. Hope in the promises of God is the fertilizer our shriveling friends lack. Instead of seeing only what is possible in the natural, they need to focus on the potential God has for their lives.

What do you say to your friends when they're feeling down and almost out? Do you look to their surrounding circumstances to point out a few glimmers of hope, or do you remind them of God's promises? In order to be suppliers of hope in your friends' lives, you need to be a person of hope yourself, knowing and believing the promises of God. Your encouragement of hope must come from your own experiences of finding hope in God's promises. Only then can you truly pass hope on to others.

Sometimes we only recognize our need for hope in God when we can find no other way out. That's what happened to my husband Rich and the other directors of the rescue mission in our county. Several years ago the mission began building a new facility. It was being constructed debt free. When it was 95-percent completed, the builder announced he was off the original cost schedule by an additional $30,000.

That evening the board of directors held an emergency meeting to discuss possible alternatives. They couldn't find any. Donors had already given sacrificially. Contacting them again for more money was out of the question. The individual board members were not in a position to take out a loan of this amount. Most of them were doing well to pay their own bills. Any cash they had stashed away already had been given to the cause.

The one thing they did have, however, was the belief that God wanted them to build this new structure without going into debt. That left them with only one direction to turn: upward. They fell on their knees and placed their hope in the Lord. Everyone in the room could identify with Moses when the only assurance he had was God's reminder, "Is the Lord's arm too short? You will now see whether or not what I say will come true for you" (Numbers 11:23). That night the board of directors ended the meeting believing the Chairman of the board—Father God—would provide a miracle.

He didn't waste any time in doing so. When the secretary arrived early the next morning to open the front door, she found an old shoe box on the front step. Removing the lid, she discovered the box was full of old gold and silver coins. Neither a note nor a call of explanation was ever received. It was amazing that someone would leave such a treasure unprotected in one of the poorest, most crime-ridden areas of the county. It was a miracle that it had not been taken.

The second miracle came later in the day. The precious metals broker valued the coins at $30,056, just the amount needed to finish the construction! Rich and the other directors were not disappointed by their hope in God's Word.

In order to fill our lives with godly hope, we must fill our hearts and minds with God's Word Paul wrote, "For everything that was written in the past was written to teach us, so that through endurance and the encouragement of the Scriptures we might have hope" (Romans 15:4). It's important to spend time in God's Word daily.

Some people think that reading good books *about* the promises of God is the same as studying God's Word. This is not the case. Jesus says clearly in the Gospel of John that it is His Words that produce life (John 15:1-8). Though it is helpful to read what others have learned by sitting at the feet of Jesus, the Bible is our primary source of godly hope.

Sharing Hope with Our Friends

One of the most effective ways to share godly hope with our disappointed and despairing friends is through words of appreciation. Thoughtful words appeal to the little, blue forget-me-not in all of us. Everybody responds positively when they are noticed and appreciated.

My friend Patti told me that sometimes a friend will send her a card with a Scripture verse and a note of appreciation for no particular reason. She saves these messages of hope. In her times of weariness she pulls one out and reads it. That's the nice thing about putting your appreciation in writing instead of just sharing it over the phone. Your friends can pull them out whenever they need a lift. Just a brief note with a word of hope can be a stabilizing factor when a friend's world is turning upside down.

When traumatic events occur in our friends' lives, they need wheelbarrows full of hope. That's what the disciples experienced when Jesus, whom they loved and trusted, suddenly left them after His resurrection and ascension One day they had an intimate relationship

with Him, and the next day He was gone. We hav
perienced the same sense of loss through the deatl
a loved one, a divorce, or when a close friend moves
away. Traumatic events send people searching for the
shelter of relationships. The disciples huddled together
behind closed doors in fear. They were imprisoned by
the cares of this world, feeling trapped and alone. But
then Jesus appeared on the scene with the hope of
peace.

Often in the midst of distress people run together,
hoping to find comfort and security in their relationships. That's when we need to communicate through
our words and actions the promises of God which will
see them through.

At other times, when life is less hectic, we need
to share hope and encouragement by expressing our appreciation for no particular reason. Our friends need to
feel special. Some of them have felt unappreciated since
their childhood, like they really don't matter to anyone.
If your friends feel like losers, make them feel like win-
ners. Let your acts of appreciation be a demonstration of
your love. Sharing an encouraging word or deed with a
friend will add so much to the life of your garden.
When you generously heap gratitude on a friend, you
will receive the blessing of a more intimate relationship
in return.

My friend Charlie is a working mom who did not
want her children in day care. Seeing she had a need I
could easily fill, I offered to pick her children up after
school with my three daughters. Every day her children
and mine do homework together.

As a way of saying thank you, Charlie brings
over big boxes of grapes on her way to work in the
morning. Or she drops off a couple bags of carrots all

cleaned and sliced for the kids' snacks. Or she and her husband take our girls for a weekend so Rich and I can spend some time together alone. They look for opportunities to show their appreciation.

Someone else I know who is serving a friend in a similar way feels terribly used because no gestures of gratitude are shown. Why do some people fail to show appreciation? I believe it's a lack of teaching. Children should be taught from their youth to sit down and write thank you notes for gifts received or the hospitality of a friend who invited them to sleep over.

Children also need to learn to show appreciation to their parents for all the little things they do. The other night, my daughter Amy invited some other young teenagers to our house for dinner and then to Solid Rock night, our church's youth meeting. After the events of the evening, Amy came over to me and with a warm hug said, "Mom, thanks for dinner and for everything else too." Amy said it all. She will never know how much her little thank you means to me. My teenage daughter demonstrated she had learned the lesson of appreciation well. Teaching your children to be appreciative will equip them to be messengers of hope in their relationships as they grow older.

Whether you have been taught as a child to show appreciation or not, it's never too late to learn. Many people, however, think of showing appreciation as paying someone back for a favor. That's not appreciation; it's paying a debt. We need to begin thinking of appreciation as an act above and beyond the normal or the expected. Sometimes it's just acknowledging the fact that someone has done something for you they didn't have to do. If every act of kindness was followed by an act of appreciation, can you imagine how much more encouraged we would be to show kind consideration? We must never take our beautiful garden of friends for granted.

We need to become more aware of the people around us. Take a minute to do something that shows appreciation. Go the extra mile to let someone know you care. Sometimes it doesn't require anything big like a long letter or a major commitment. Maybe it's just writing a card or a brief note or picking up the phone and sending a bouquet of flowers. Sometimes our appreciation is in the form of a spoken word of encouragement that directs your friends to the promises of God. This is how we fertilize our friends with hope.

I know firsthand. I just lost 38 pounds. That's after I already lost 30 pounds, then gained back 35. One day the Lord helped me realize that He had called me to a life-style of obedience, not to a fluctuating scale of dress sizes. I had to maintain my proper weight for the rest of my life.

My greatest help came from friends who believed in me and prayed for me. They expressed hope that I could take the weight off again and keep it off when others were probably whispering, "Maybe she will; maybe she won't. You know how she loves to eat. Besides, Rich will love her anyway, thunder thighs and all." I knew what they were thinking. I had passed the same judgment on myself for years. But my hope-filled friends helped me get beyond my self-doubt and positively expect the promise of God to be fulfilled: "I can do everything through [Christ] who gives me strength" (Philippians 4:13).

It's very important for us to inspire supernatural hope in everyone we meet by speaking God's promises rather than perpetuating the comments or actions of man. This is how we lay the foundation for success instead of despair in our friends. Hope nurtures our friends to blossom into fruitfulness, especially when the fertilizer of hope is blended with the water of faith.

Faith-filled Friendships

If you've ever read the instructions on a bag of fertilizer, you know that once the fertilizer is spread around the plant, the soil must be turned and watered deeply. The idea is to get the fertilizer down to the taproot where it will nourish and enrich the plant.

So it is with hope. Just as fertilizer needs water to force the nutrients into the soil, so God's fertilizer of hope must reach our friends' taproots of belief before they can blossom abundantly. Hope by itself is non-productive. Alone it causes no change in the spiritual or physical realm. Hope requires the second half of our prescription for fruitfulness: Love always trusts.

This means love always believes, always has faith. Paul wasn't saying that a Christian filled with love is so naive as to believe everything he hears and sees. Instead, faith means we put our confidence in or rely on the promises of God today. Faith must be in the present tense.

So how do we know we are trusting God to carry us through every difficult situation in our relationships? Our actions will prove it (James 2:17,18). Faith must be accompanied by obedient, loving action in our relationships (1 John 4:16,21; 5:3,4). This guarantees our victory. Love will prevail in our lives and the lives of those around us when we stand firm in faith during life's circumstances. When we truly trust God we will continue to obey Him and respond lovingly toward others, even when the relationships and circumstances don't turn out the way we planned.

Sarah's story is a beautiful example of faith and hope in action in the midst of relationship difficulties. Two weeks before their wedding, Sarah's fiance Tom was told he had cancer. Believing for a miracle, they decided to marry anyway. For four years Tom endured great pain, undergoing every type of treatment and surgery available. His condition continued to deteriorate.

Sarah's days were consumed with her intense management job, which often required her to take work home. Nights were spent taking care of Tom, whom she grew to love more than life itself. Sarah was the only source of support for Tom and his eight-year-old son, and the burden seemed overwhelming. To help share the load, Tom's mother moved in. Though this offered some relief, it did not slow down the monthly stream of medical bills. Tom's mother consoled Sarah with the fact that Sarah was the beneficiary on Tom's life insurance policy.

As time passed, however, there was a marked change in the attitude of Sarah's mother-in-law. Weeks before Tom's death, she convinced him, the family, and their church that Sarah was cheating on her husband. The woman even went as far as to file a police report accusing Sarah of contributing to Tom's deteriorating condition through her infidelity.

Sarah was crushed. Having to forgive such a lie was almost unbearable. Yet she continued to trust and obey God and act in love in her relationship with Tom and his mother. Finally after a long, painful battle with cancer, Tom died.

Sarah insisted no corners be cut in the expense of the funeral. Tom's mother agreed. She assured the funeral director the cost would be easily covered by the benefits from Tom's life insurance policy paid to Sarah.

Sarah's mother, a faithful woman of God who has a national reputation for walking in love, spoke at Tom's funeral. Her sermon was about the path through the valley of the shadow of death mentioned in Psalm 23:4. She told the 200 people who attended that the pathway through trials is love. Those who choose to walk this path get safely through the dark valley. Those who ignore the path of love stay behind.

Soon after Tom was laid to rest, Sarah was shocked to learn that Tom's mother had named herself the beneficiary on Tom's policy two weeks before his death. What's more, the woman felt no responsibility to share the benefits with Sarah. The expenses of Tom's medical care, and now his funeral, fell completely on her shoulders. She felt her faith being pushed to the breaking point. She wanted to give up on God.

Sarah's mother consoled her with a startling statement: "Sarah, if your life is not greatly improved one year from now, may God strike me dead." She was deeply convinced of God's goodness and that His principles for walking in love work. Her strong conviction caught Sarah's attention.

That very night Sarah met a precious man of God, whom she married six months later. Three days after her mother's bold statement, Sarah was informed by the employee benefits department at her office that she was the beneficiary of a special life insurance policy available to managers and their families. As a result of Tom's death, Sarah received an unexpected check for $53,000. She was able to pay her outstanding bills and make a down payment on a home she would share with her new husband.

Sarah's faithfulness would have been futile without her hope in God. Neither could she have sustained her walk with the Lord through this difficult time without His hope in her heart. Her loving mother was an instrument in her life to encourage the hope she needed.

Just as fertilizer and water must go hand in hand in order to produce vital plant growth, so faith and hope are the necessary ingredients for vibrant friendships that can withstand the adversities of life. God is a trustworthy and awesome God. He wants us to be fully saturated with faith in Him and hope in His promises. The more we trust Him, the deeper our roots go. The deeper our roots, the stronger we become. And as others see how our trust in God sustains us through conflicts, they will be encouraged to trust Him too.

CHAPTER SIXTEEN

Persevering Through the Chilly Winds of Change

Sometimes the frigid north winds of discord or disinterest blow through our garden of friends. A relationship that once glowed warm with love and friendship gradually cools for no apparent reason. Or someone suddenly gives you the cold shoulder and stops speaking to you. How do you respond in a relationship when the temperature drops and a killer frost threatens to wipe it out?

It is often during the cold blasts of the north wind in our relationships that we get a clearer picture of the last attribute on Paul's checklist in 1 Corinthians 13:4-7: Love always perseveres. To persevere means to hang in there courageously during suffering, trials, and temptations. Instead of depending on a lot of support from others to get us through, perseverance requires more personal involvement. This is a test of your faith and character, a test you may have to endure by trusting in the Lord alone. In fact, the very people you would ordinarily depend on for support may be the ones God uses to perform the test. Oftentimes they are the people you trust the most.

A Test of Trust

Ten years ago our friend Patrick moved to Chicago and joined the prestigious law firm of two other Christian attorneys, Duane and Jerry. The Lord clearly revealed to Patrick that he was to trust Him in this partnership situation. By trusting the Lord, Patrick released his Christian partners from his expectations for their relationship.

After eight years of close friendship and partnership with Duane and Jerry, Patrick's warm relationship with them was put to a chilly test. So was his ability to trust God in the relationship. The original profit sharing formula had become outdated over the years due to the growth of the firm. Patrick had increased the firm's profitability by 30 percent, but only a small fraction of the increase was reflected in his earnings.

When Patrick approached his partners concerning the inequity of the arrangement, they disagreed with him. Patrick knew, however, that Duane and Jerry believed they were being fair and that they were doing right according to their original agreement. Since his trust was in God, Patrick did not jump to his own defense or press the issue. He decided to persevere and let God sustain him through the chilly blast that threatened to divide the partnership. He told Duane and Jerry that he was going to trust God to help them resolve their differences over the profit sharing dilemma.

In time the Lord was faithful to speak clearly to Patrick's partners. Duane and Jerry developed an outstanding profit sharing formula that more accurately reflected Patrick's contribution to the firm. Through this ordeal Patrick's relationship with Duane and Jerry also benefited. It became stronger. Patrick was grateful to God for the growth he experienced as a result of persevering the chilly test by trusting God.

Trust is an important factor in friendships. But the primary object of our trust is not people but God. In the Psalms we read, "It is better to trust in the Lord than to put confidence in man" (118:8, NKJV). If our trust in our friends is greater than our trust in God, we violate the intimacy God desires in our relationship with Him. The Scriptures issue a strong warning to those who misplace their trust: "Woe to those who call evil good and good evil, who put darkness for light and light for darkness, who put bitter for sweet and sweet for bitter. Woe to those who are wise in their own eyes and clever in their own sight" (Isaiah 5:20,21).

In any relationship we must trust God even more than we trust people. Why? Because in a conflict, your friends may believe they are being fair in what they are doing and what they demand from you. The book of Proverbs says, "Every way of a man is right in his own eyes" (Proverbs 21:2, NKJV). We all tend to believe that our perspective and way of doing things is right. But only God has perfect perspective. That's why He's the only one we can fully trust to see us through a difficult situation. When we trust in ourselves or others instead of God, we become vulnerable to our own imperfect schemes.

Calmed by Peace

God's peace in the chilly trials that blow into your

friendships is directly related to your trust in God. When you choose to trust God in your relationships, you will experience His peace. If you fail to trust Him, and put your trust either in yourself or others, God's peace will elude you.

Trusting God means you believe He will take care of all the obstacles in your life, including difficulties in your garden of friends. You can measure the amount of trust you are exercising by the amount of peace you are experiencing during a relationship problem. If you allow yourself to be anxious, mad, or hurt or to desire the worst for the person you're struggling with, you are telling the Lord you really don't trust His ability to solve your problem. When you take the problem-solving responsibility in your relationships into your own hands, you block the flow of God's peace to your situation.

The world teaches us to think of ourselves as loners on life's battlegrounds. We're surrounded by messages like, "You're all by yourself when others are against you, so take matters into your own hands and give it your best shot." But the world's perspective stands in opposition to God's Word. In Proverbs we read, "Trust in the Lord with all your heart and lean not on your own understanding; in all your ways acknowledge him, and he will make your paths straight" (3:5,6). We must realize that the only way to victory and peace in our relationship conflicts is from trusting the Lord.

Exercising trust in God and experiencing His peace in the midst of a chilly conflict doesn't always mean we know what the outcome will be. Trusting God is like driving at night down a dark highway. The headlights only shine a short distance ahead. Our confidence and peace comes from knowing that, although our understanding is limited, God sees everything clearly. He knows the end from the beginning. And if we trust Him even when we can't see very far ahead, He will lead us safely where we need to go.

The Friendship to Be Guarded above All Others

The perseverance of unconditional love is often put to the supreme test in the relationship of a husband and wife. By God's design, husband and wife are to be forever friends. Jesus said, "They are no longer two, but one. Therefore what God has joined together, let man not separate" (Matthew 19:6). Sometimes perseverance in a marriage requires the dogged determination to obey God instead of allowing the cold north wind of incompatibility or lack of love to build a wall of ice between marriage partners.

Many years ago our marriage hit rock bottom. Feelings of love between Rich and me basically disintegrated. I had saved up a lot of unforgiveness and anger from my childhood and dumped it all on Rich. Of course, he didn't want it. His reaction brought everything to what I thought was the breaking point. But things got worse in our life. I was in a serious car accident. Our dear friend Keith Green and two of his children were killed in a plane crash. I could only wonder what was next. Little did I know we were about to endure one of the harshest winter storms of our life.

Our world was crumbling around us, but nobody realized it. Ours still looked like a secure, successful marriage. Yet we were at a point of decision: Either break the tie that bound us and end the life we began together or be obedient to God and persevere. Believe me, for awhile the former looked a lot easier than the latter. I cried out to God, "Do whatever you have to do

208 • *Chilly Winds of Change*

to make me the person you really want me to be. But God, please help me. I can't take any more."

We knew the Lord didn't want us to seek counseling with friends or a professional. Instead, He directed us to start a fellowship group in our home. God wanted us to start counseling others. Even in the midst of our own blizzard of difficulties, we couldn't leave our friends out in the cold, out of our life. The Lord still required us to stand among the friends in our garden and water them with faith while we were withstanding our own blizzard.

Though we cared for others out of obedience, we felt so helpless, so icy cold toward each other. What did we have to offer others? God assured us that through giving to others we would receive our healing. He was right. So many times our needs are met by ministering to others. God gave Rich and I answers for others that clearly applied to our life together. The more we persevered and applied God's Word to our relationship, the warmer the temperature became between us. And from the rubble God reconstructed a solid, wonderful marriage on the sure foundation of Jesus Christ.

Persevering to Maturity

Enduring an arctic blast in your friendship or marriage leads to growth and enables you to encourage others. No matter how long and cold winter gets, it's always followed by spring. The tests and trials of the stinging cold are part of God's growing process. Unconditional love perseveres through the cold winds of winter and eventually welcomes the growth and fruitfulness of spring. James writes, "Consider it pure joy, my brothers, whenever you face trials of many kinds, because you know that the testing of your faith develops perseverance. Perseverance must finish its work so that you may be mature and complete, not lacking anything" (James 1:2-4). Regardless of how cold things get between us and a friend, we are to take on an "attitude of gratitude." Be creative: Ask God for insights that will enable you to persevere to maturity.

God allows trials in our relationships for one reason: to produce mature, enduring love in our lives for Jesus and others. If we choose to walk in the 12 attributes of unconditional love in 1 Corinthians 13:4-7, the character of Jesus will spring forth in us. Jesus does not touch our lives and leave us unchanged. The power of God's love in our hearts makes a tangible difference. Our once sparse gardens will burst forth in healthy relationships.

CHAPTER SEVENTEEN

The
Master
Gardener

As we have taken a close look at God's checklist for nurturing a healthy garden of friends, hopefully you have been affirmed in some steps you are already taking as a friend. For example, perhaps you recognize areas where God has helped you practice patience and kindness with a friend who is sometimes difficult to be around. Or maybe you realize that you have been fairly consistent at nurturing some of your friends with the fertilizer of hope and the water of faith. In some respects you're encouraged that you're on the way to becoming a loving, nurturing friend to those God has planted in your garden.

On the other hand, you have no doubt identified some other areas of friendship where you need to grow. Perhaps you are aware of some wrongs others have done

212 • *The Master Gardener*

to you that need to be pruned away with the shears of forgiveness. Maybe for the first time you see some of the "wild bunch" members of your family as potential friends you need to nurture. Or possibly you recognize barriers of prejudice or pride that have prevented some people from being planted in your life.

First, realize that you are being lovingly tended by the Master Gardener. Isaiah wrote, "Sing about a fruitful vineyard: I, the Lord, watch over it; I water it continually. I guard it day and night so that no one may harm it" (27:2,3). You are planted in His garden. He loves you and cares about your growth and fruitfulness. Even His pruning in our lives is for our fruitfulness (John 15:2; Hebrews 12:11). The Master Gardener is committed to nurturing you in His garden and enabling you as a loving gardener in the lives of your friends.

Furthermore, you are tapped into Jesus Christ, your model and resource for being a loving friend. Jesus said, "I am the vine; you are the branches. If a man remains in me, and I in him, he will bear much fruit; apart from me you can do nothing" (John 15:5). Jesus is the source of all the love attributes listed in 1 Corinthians 13:4-7. As you allow your friendship with Him to flourish, your capacity for growing as a loving, nurturing friend will increase.

Second, realize that growth and change doesn't happen overnight. Any gardener knows that cultivating and maintaining a flourishing garden takes time and commitment. You can pick up the phone and be talking to a friend thousands of miles away in seconds. You can push a few buttons on your microwave and cook a meal in minutes. But even in this age of instant everything, you can't make a flower grow any faster than God has programmed it to grow. Your responsibility is to plant, fertilize, water, and cultivate, but then you must wait for the growth which only God can give.

Don't be discouraged if you are not yet a fully blossomed friend. The Master Gardener is at work in your life, and you are growing. But maturity takes time. And don't be disappointed if you have found areas in your life where you are not yet an expert at cultivating the friends in your garden. Continue to learn from the Master Gardener, and apply what you learn in your relationships. Commit yourself to being a good friend and cultivating loving friendships, then allow time for God to grow you to maturity. The love you show to your friends is a reflection of your friendship with God. It is in that reflection that you catch a glimpse of your unique potential as an individual in God's creation.

Third, remember your goal in all your efforts to be a friend and cultivate friendships. We sometimes live as if our goal is to fill our garden with as many friends as possible in the years God grants us.

But it's not how many friends we accumulate; it's what happens in the individual lives of the friends we have that's important. Your goal is not to have more and more friends, even though there's nothing wrong with cultivating a large garden of friends. Your goal is to be the best friend possible to the friends you have. Your life is significant because you are walking with the Master Gardener, expressing His love to those around you, and pointing them to Him. This is your destiny, whether you tend a small garden or several acres of friends.

One day you shall see the reward of your investment in the lives of people. You will gather in the presence of the Master Gardener and present yourself to Him as a member of His glorious bridal bouquet. Your fulfillment will be complete as you hear Him say, "Well done, good and faithful servant! You have been faithful with a few things; I will put you in charge of many things. Come and share your master's happiness!" (Matthew 25:21). And you will experience utter joy as He pronounces you His forever friend.

Notes and
Recommended Reading

Notes

Chapter 1—Are You in a Weed Patch?
1. Charles L. Wallis, ed., *The Treasure Chest* (Maplewood, NJ: Hammond Inc., 1965), p. 99.

Chapter 2—How Does Your Garden Grow?
1. I am indebted to Dick Foth, a minister who teaches relationship seminars all over the United States, for his insights into the four parts of a friendship. Some of the ideas in this book are adapted from his tape series, *Marriage Enrichment '91*.

Chapter 4—The Special Circle of Friends
1. "Men Make Strides in Closing Emotional Gaps," *USA Today*, August 26, 1991, p. 4D.
2. Ibid.
3. H. Norman Wright, *The Power of a Parent's Words* (Ventura, CA: Regal Books, 1991), p. 149, 150.
4. Gary Smalley, *The Key to Your Child's Heart* (Dallas: Word Publishing, 1984), p. 64.
5. Wright, *The Power of a Parent's Words*, p. 54, 55.

Chapter 5—A Bouquet for the Friends of Friends
1. W.E. Vine, *An Expository Dictionary of New Testament Words* (Nashville, TN: Thomas Nelson Publishers), pp. 150, 151.

Chapter 6—Dealing with Differences
1. For a more complete description of the strengths and weaknesses of these four personality types, please refer to Florence Littauer, *How to Get Along with Difficult People* (Eugene, OR: Harvest House Publishers, 1984), pp. 172-175.
2. Ibid., p. 38.
3. Ibid., p. 101.

Chapter 7—Why Do We Treat Friends like Weeds?
1. Neil Clark Warren, *Make Anger Your Ally* (Brentwood, TN: Wolgemuth and Hyatt, Publishers, 1990), adapted from p. 96.
2. Ibid., p. 100.
3. Ibid.

Chapter 10—Be a Giver
1. Lewis B. Smedes, *A Pretty Good Person* (San Francisco: Harper and Row, Publishers, 1990), p. 13.

Chapter 11—Don't Let Your Anger Cut Down Your Friends
1. Neil Clark Warren, *Make Anger Your Ally* (Brentwood, TN: Wolgemuth and Hyatt, Publishers, 1990), p. 3.
2. Ibid., pp. 17,18.

3. Ibid., p. 76.
4. Ibid., adapted from pp. 179, 180.
5. Ibid.

Chapter 12—Prune Away the Dead Leaves
1. W.E. Vine, *An Expository Dictionary of New Testament Words* (Nashville, TN: Thomas Nelson Publishers), p. 1139.
2. Chuck Smith from his Bible-study tape series, *1 Corinthians 13*.
3. Neil Clark Warren, *Making Anger Your Ally* (Brentwood, TN: Wolgemuth and Hyatt, Publishers, 1990), pp. 187, 188.

Chapter 14—Keep Your Friends Covered
1. W.E. Vine, *An Expository Dictionary of New Testament Words* (Nashville, TN: Thomas Nelson Publishers), p. 94.
2. H. Clay Trumbull, *The Blood Covenant* (Kirkwood, MO: Impact Books, 1975), n.p.
3. From the lecture notes of Dr. C. Peter Wagner, "How to Have a Prayer Ministry," Church Growth and Prayer series.
4. Barbara M. Bowen, *Strange Scriptures that Perplex the Western Mind* (Grand Rapids, MI: William B. Eerdmans Publishing Co., 1940), adapted from pp. 31, 32

Recommended Reading

Anderson, Neil T. *Making Anger Your Ally*. Eugene, OR: Harvest House Publishing, 1990

Dalbey, Gordon. *Healing of the Masculine Soul*. Dallas: Word Publishing, 1988.

Harley, William F., Jr., Ph.D. *His Needs, Her Needs*. Old Tappan, NJ: Fleming H. Revell Co., Publishers, 1986.

Littauer, Florence. *How to Get Along with Difficult People*. Eugene, OR: Harvest House Publishers, 1984.

Marshall, Tom. *Right Relationships*. Chichester, England: Sovereign World, 1989.

Smalley, Gary. *The Key to Your Child's Heart*. Dallas: Word Publishing, 1984.

Smalley, Gary and Trent, John, Dr. *The Language of Love*. Pomona, CA: Focus on the Family Publishing, 1988.

Warren, Neil Clark. Ph.D. *Making Anger Your Ally*. Brentwood, TN: Wolgemuth & Hyatt, Publishers, Inc., 1990.

Wright, H. Norman. *The Power of a Parent's Words*. Ventura, CA: Regal Books, 1991